Paula —

Saluting your passion for organic food + farming,

Best,

High Up in the Rolling Hills

A Living on the Land

Peter Finch

iUniverse, Inc.
Bloomington

HIGH UP IN THE ROLLING HILLS
A LIVING ON THE LAND

Copyright © 2013 Peter Finch.

All rights reserved. No part of this book may be used or reproduced by any means, graphic, electronic, or mechanical, including photocopying, recording, taping or by any information storage retrieval system without the written permission of the publisher except in the case of brief quotations embodied in critical articles and reviews.

iUniverse books may be ordered through booksellers or by contacting:

iUniverse
1663 Liberty Drive
Bloomington, IN 47403
www.iuniverse.com
1-800-Authors (1-800-288-4677)

Because of the dynamic nature of the Internet, any web addresses or links contained in this book may have changed since publication and may no longer be valid. The views expressed in this work are solely those of the author and do not necessarily reflect the views of the publisher, and the publisher hereby disclaims any responsibility for them.

Any people depicted in stock imagery provided by Thinkstock are models, and such images are being used for illustrative purposes only.

Certain stock imagery © Thinkstock.

Front cover image by Nina Keogh
www.ninakeogh.com

ISBN: 978-1-4759-8585-6 (sc)
ISBN: 978-1-4759-8587-0 (hc)
ISBN: 978-1-4759-8586-3 (e)

Printed in the United States of America.

iUniverse rev. date: 4/18/2013

To my dad, Jack Finch, for his tireless humanitarian activism;

*and to my mum, Mary Finch, née Mullins,
for her endless unflappable goodness.*

*I miss you both and cherish the memories you
gave me, many of which are recalled here.*

Table Of Contents

Preface ix
Chapter 1   Preambles in Childhood and Youth 1
Chapter 2   Migrating to the New World 15
Chapter 3   A Sense of Arrival 27
Chapter 4   Into a New Millennium 35
Chapter 5   Echinacea Planting 61
Chapter 6   Co-operative Years 71
Chapter 7   A Health Scare 81
Chapter 8   Trust Nature 93
Chapter 9   Hoop Houses 103
Chapter 10 Into a Second Decade 117
Chapter 11 Looking Back, Moving Forward 139
Epilogue 173
Appendix 179

Preface

NORTHUMBERLAND HILLS, ONTARIO, SPRING 2013

The world beyond my immediate horizon of rolling hills stretches to dominions that are no longer so distant. In fact, they seem to be pressing in on us. The gluttonous bankers are mercilessly after their pound of flesh. Those that govern us are running scared from the runaway train of obligations. They would like to rein us in with the empty promise of protection from mythical forces of evil. Military dinosaurs plot their next "humanitarian" assault on a demonized state, using innocent civilians as cannon fodder. And, of course, corporate connivers continue, scarcely regulated and so unabated, their plunder and perversion of the natural world.

    Stretched to that same southern horizon are fields of food and meadows of medicine, a cedar grove dropping off to a wetland with an infant stream snaking across it, sloping up beyond to mixed woodlands of pine, birch, maple, oak and then open fields, tree-lined ridges, strings of towns, the expanse of Lake Ontario, and the length and breadth of the United States of America. We are Finches perched here, at home and at peace up in the hills, in tune with the seasons as they do their swirling, mesmerizing dance.

In student days, I recorded muddy, often brooding ramblings in my five-year diary, a catalogue of youthful desire, cravings, insecurity, hunger for experience. It was supplanted by endless lists and chronicles as I vainly sought to keep pace with the years as they sped by in a blur. I drafted, procured, published and peddled maps and satellite images portraying our world in varying guises. Then, Web sites and two blogs have given channels of expression to my passions for maps, glass sculpture, nature as muse, food and farming. As life in the rolling hills unfolded, the soil, seeds, plants, harvests and farmers markets took a firm grip on my spirit. Here and now, I record pieces of this puzzle and a period still unfolding of what are hopefully middle years for me.

Passion remains, anticipation abounds, and their bond strengthens. I feel comfortable in my past, good in my bones, strong in my heart, bright in my mind, positive in my outlook, and up for the challenges that lie ahead. My partner and I seek out nature, food, and love uncompromisingly as we are privileged perchance to explore and roam lands both near and far. A romantic at heart, always was, ever will be, I gain inspiration from the vision of people who act as catalysts, who elevate us and create belonging in this world that we so fleetingly inhabit.

I

Preambles in Childhood and Youth

I was born into this world in the mid-1950s, and my father, Jack, endured the grind of commuting daily by car to "the Big Smoke," the hectic city of London, to work for an advertising company.

Peter and Dad in front of an advertisement for Bovril in London

His job took him travelling all over the country in his capacity as outdoor advertising site manager. After long days of work, he found time and energy to devote to the depressed and suicidal as a volunteer for the Samaritans. He seemed to be always away except on cherished weekends.

In my youth, Dad envied my footloose travels, my wanderlust. As a loving father, he always wanted me to settle into a cosy routine, into a safe marriage, into a secure career. He was always coming up with new ideas, especially for my fledgling map business and gardening pursuits. I, in turn, envied his flying and gliding exploits; he told me that there is nothing to match the feeling of hearing only the whoosh of the wind when gliding free. I also envied his bravura in taking on challenges and truly getting things done. I took on his passion for gardening, sports, poetry, maps and music, and some of his humanitarian character couldn't help but rub off on me.

In flight training in the Royal Air Force in his late teens, Jack was transported into another realm by gliding, as he later wrote in "The Untrodden Highways":

Up in the blue-grey realms of sky,
Unconfined by earthly constraint,
You can move in all dimensions,
In those wide untrodden highways.

You're free to wheel or loop or drift.
You can roll, climb, spin or hover.
You can dive like a young eagle.
You can soar like a carefree lark.

Who cares if it's gloomy on earth?
Climb through the cloud to dazzling light.
Fling your craft in wide open space
In that kingdom of far beyond.

As he wrote this, his world was young, as were his comrades. They all trooped off to war, and many were destined not to return to their normal lives, cut off in their prime, or their loved ones at home. Jack was left with a sense of guilt and a lingering grief that never left him despite his great humour and bubbly joviality in all his long years.

I have always been grateful that mandatory military service was abolished in my homeland when I was in my late teens. It was not for me and, had I been German and faced with the choice between military service, social service and moving to West Berlin, I would certainly have opted against the military option. Luckily for me, camaraderie was readily available from sports and school, and I could honour my civic duty without bearing arms.

My mother, born Mary Mullins, grew up in Oxford, where she was to become head girl at Oxford Girls' School on New Inn Hall Street, with just a brick wall separating her school from my university college, St Peter's, where I was to study some 35 years later. Mum worked for a while as secretary to E. F. Schumacher, who achieved fame for his marvellously insightful book *Small Is Beautiful*, which my sister Jill gave me in my late teens. Later in life when I threw myself into organic-food growing, the principles Schumacher espoused truly took on deep meaning for me.

As the Second World War came to an end, Mary wrote "One Day when We Were Young," on October 7, 1945. It was her story of young love and the painful decisions young lovers had to make immediately after the war, despite the promises of peace. She was 22 at the time.

> One Sunday when a young girl and a young boy awoke
> to find one of those rare glorious days in October, they

decided to set out for a walk. The haze was lifting and the blue-grey sky was gradually growing blue. They set off, hand in hand, with her dog very pleased at knowing he was being taken for a walk. Now the warmth of the sun was burning their backs, now caressing their faces. As they were climbing to the top of Shotover Plain the young man, who was a flight lieutenant pilot, said that he had to decide by the next morning whether he was going to volunteer for eighteen months' ground staff duties or eighteen months with a chance of flying duties, with a possibility of the latter being lengthened to four years. Here was one of the millions of problems that were having to be solved by so many men and women, now that the fighting side of the war was o'er. As they discussed this view and that, they found they had come to the end of their climb and were now walking over Shotover Plain. The conversation had brought them closer to each other than they had ever been before in the comparatively short time since they had met each other. The magnificent morning and the beautiful surroundings made such an awe-inspiring atmosphere. And so they strolled, roaming down one field to view a copse that lay in a dell, ahead of them. The sun emphasized the green, brown and golden tints of the leaves, and away in the distance, the hills rolled into space. As they went on their way, they stopped to admire a group of beech trees with their smooth slender trunks, and their eyes looked upward to see the blue sky peeping through the dense foliage above them. Everywhere they walked they crunched over the fallen multi-coloured leaves. The red berries were thick on the bushes. Now and again, they stopped to eat a few blackberries that were warm from the sun. Before they started to descend from the Plain, they scanned the wonderful view that was spread before them. It seemed that for a few brief moments they had managed to get out and rise above the world they belonged to … And so they left this vision they had shared and returned to the world below.

The miracle of life began for me, at home, Saplings in Mill Lane, Chalfont St. Giles, Buckinghamshire, England, in May 1956 at 9:15 in the morning, just after my two sisters, Jill and Jenny, had left to walk to school. The town of my birth had been home to famed poet and statesman John Milton some three hundred years before. His picturesque cottage, where he penned his epic *Paradise Lost* while escaping the Great Plague of London in the years 1664–1666, remains intact.

As a youngster, I didn't really appreciate that we lived just 20 miles from London since I was rarely exposed to the city. I inhabited an innocent realm symbolized by our sumac tree, weeping willow ("I'm the king of the castle; get down you dirty rascal") and leafy lanes we walked along to school (like Dodd's Lane, where I was scared by the appearance of "black ghosts," or nuns). We were warned to keep away from the gypsy camp on the edge of the woods, and so curiosity naturally drew us to it.

Dad was captain of Fencibles Cricket Club in Amersham, Buckinghamshire. Their ground was rather plain, and I used to long for the spectacular setting of the yearly Old Albanians away fixture in St. Albans. During the match, my mates and I made a great escape into a wooded dell which was formed into a bowl at one end of the cricket pitch. I latched on to the other boys, and off we ran into the woods for hours of self-made entertainment and exploration of imagined worlds. These were part of our virtual fantasy world all those decades before video games and Harry Potter. I can't begin to think what we got up to, but we'd return at teatime all scratched up, muddy-kneed, sheepish and breathless. After a sausage-sandwich supper served up by the cricket ladies (to whom my mum would proudly introduce me as her "son and heir") and being teased by Albert Cox (who left me gaping when he would briefly light his hairy chest with a match), we'd roll on home. As my family descended the hill in our trusty Morris Minor and crossed the stream in Mill Lane on the last leg home, in the dark, we'd all belt out our song:

> Here we are again, happy as can be,
> All good friends and jolly good company.
> Never mind the weather, never mind the rain,
> Now we're all together, whoops she goes again.

An old music-hall song, this ditty was the perfect expression of jollity and belonging. In later years, even into her late eighties in a nursing home, Mum would beam as she heard this tune.

Walks with my sisters to nearby farms and a trip to Whipsnade Zoo led me to announce one day at the age of 4 that, when I grew up, I wanted to be a farmer with five lions on my farm. The seed was already planted in my brain. The lions never materialized, but the farming did.

Presumably frustrated by his job, Dad took on part-time gardening jobs tending the rambling back garden of a client in Gerrards Cross, planting flowers in a car-sales display in Marlow (where the pungent aroma from the steaming brewery nauseated me), and caring for long flower beds along the frontage of a noisy and smelly plastics factory in Slough. I was privileged to help water the plants and dig beds, being treated to hot savoury steak pies at the transport caf en route.

When I was 7, our family made a big move. Dad officially quit the rat race, and he and Mum became joint wardens of Little Pond House Convalescent Home for Children in Tilford, Surrey. Into thin air went the nuclear three-child family, walks through the woods to school and weekends of cricket. For several years I cycled a good few miles through the lovely Surrey countryside to prep school at Barfield. When the time came for both my sisters to leave home and pursue higher education—Jill in Aberdeen and Jenny in Portsmouth—I was left to lonely nights filled with gnawing angst about the transience of life and the awful void of death as I lay awake in our cottage while my parents were over in the main house tending their flock of holidaying children. No more comforting and delicious bacon omelettes from my big sister, except on her infrequent visits home. On the flip side of the coin, as an active young boy I relished all the organized games, races and activities I shared with an ever-changing cast of playmates. The children came mostly for two-week holidays, setting aside the trials of wretched inner-city conditions of grim housing estates, poor respiratory health and, in many cases, abuse at the hands of a bullying parent or two. Many children came back for several holidays and clearly benefited from them, though I wondered how it was to have to dive back into their sad lives. Helpers to deal with the kids came from all over, and I have fond memories of lovely young women from Holland, Switzerland, and Italy. I was smitten by holidaying girls my age from Berlin, Hamburg, Paris, London and Birmingham and had innocent trysts with them, stealing wet kisses behind the ironing-room door and writing them letters, unbeknownst to my parents.

The two weeks I spent on a Mediterranean cruise at the age of 15 was the longest I had been away from home without parents.

It offered a fabulous itinerary—mostly wasted on mid-teens like me—at the fabulous price of £69, inclusive! We were 20 or so classmates, flying to Venice and joining up with the SS *Nevasa*, along with 1,000 or more other schoolchildren. From Venice, we sailed down the inky-blue Adriatic to Corfu and then docked at Piraeus for an unforgettable day in Athens. This first visit to the Acropolis and the Parthenon is an experience that remains etched vividly in my memory as a highlight of all travels (along with a visit much later in life to the Alhambra in Granada, Spain). We sailed on to Heraklion, capital of Crete, and took a bus tour to Knossos. Then it was west across the open Mediterranean to Bizerta in Tunisia. North Africa seemed highly exotic, especially the wild day trip by rickety bus to Tunis. The route of our crossing north to Italy was altered to accommodate the eruption of Stromboli on Sicily. Too bad we missed it. We docked in Napoli and had another whirlwind day scooting around Rome by bus for a few hours. Our final port of call was Livorno, base for a day trip to the Leaning Tower of Pisa, which we gleefully and dizzily mounted, as this was still allowed then.

When my parents upped sticks and moved to seaside Ramsgate in Kent to found Chilton Farmhouse Children's Holidays this same year (1971), this 15-year-old was decidedly not a happy camper. To my horror and amazement, I was told students at Chatham House Grammar School played rugby, not my beloved football. This was catastrophic, and I took to sulking around for months. I took on a newspaper round, summer bingo hall change-giving and pre-Christmas postal delivery, and, in subsequent years I spent many a boisterous, late night with school friends in Margate, pubbing and drinking beer till it overflowed out of me. I earned pocket money helping Dad on tree-planting expeditions at a sprawling garden on the clifftop overlooking the English

Channel outside Deal. He maintained a market garden, making weekly deliveries of vegetables and cut flowers to local hotels.

My first trip to Berlin was to West Berlin, at the impressionable age of 16. I was visiting my sister Jill, who at that time lived with husband Jürgen in Kreuzberg at the end of the subway line (Schlesisches Tor) at the Wall, which concealed the river Spree and the Russian Sector beyond. In the 1970s, West Berlin was a decadent, vibrant magnet, and I took many trips there over the next few years, travelling by cross-Channel ferry to Oostende in Belgium then either by train or hitched rides, even on the last tortuous leg of middle-of-the-night passport checks through security-obsessed East Germany. I worked on landscaping jobs all over the city and twice over several months as a gardener in a lovely cemetery in Schöneberg.

When working in the cemetery, I was intrigued by my peace of mind, compared with my customary irritability and ill ease in the hustle and bustle of the city. Here, I entered another realm outside the grind of my reality, and I lavished upon this realm a loving affection. What was it that empowered a cemetery to gain such a grasp on my soul? I thought I got it: The straight lines and clearly defined compartments, the oblong coffins and gravesites lent shape and pattern to my seemingly random undefined existence; the rapid, unfussy transition from life into death, the timeliness and tidiness of the whole operation of burial began to obsess me. Here I was, struggling away with my own conflicting desires and attitudes, seemingly conspiring to reduce life to one uphill struggle toward an appalling void. The appeal of a clean, painless death, suddenly giving meaning to life by comforting straight lines and clear-cut decisions, was great. Impermanence in my own life and the aura of death around me yielded to a heady air of spiritual rebirth. Physical degeneration of the body after death troubled me not at all, and I was rather lusty in handling the decayed human bones that I dug up in my occasional grave-digging. The happy discovery of an intact skull enraptured me, and the falling apart of a whole skeleton into fragments struck me as entirely natural. The cemetery was life and I the skeleton in my little box of life. I raked up endless mountains of dead leaves; it was as if the world's hair was falling out all around me, yet it all went to provide rich soil for whatever came after on that plot. A calm flowed in and waved in the wind, lingering, and drifted away. It told no lies and made me feel a mystic warmth way down inside.

Shortly after I began university studies at Oxford in 1975, I found that the rarefied atmosphere of the ivory tower was not my element. Academia was too stuffy, the syllabus too confining, and my intellectual appetite lacking. However, I do have Pot Hall (St. Peter's College) to thank for lifelong friends in Neil, Andy and Jeremy. And I did get to appreciate certain literary luminaries, electing Nietzsche, Montaigne and Molière as special authors for in-depth study. But I was a lazy oaf, skipping lectures, attempting to bluff my way through one-on-one tutorials with Reg Perman and Gilbert McKay. Reg was more easily duped, steeped in the fog of his own cocktail of arcane literature, chain-smoked cigarettes and sherry. Gilbert was much more particular, discerning and demanding. In later years, I would still jolt awake, having dreamed that I really did have to confess to Reg why I had not prepared anything for his tutorial and had been avoiding him and all studies for years.

What to do with life? Not fall into the conventional trap but find my own way. No straight-ahead path to middle management or intellectual pursuits (that graduation from Oxford prescribed) for me, but a perennial study of whatever grows naturally and is good for body and soul. I pondered becoming a gardener, park ranger or travel guide exploring foreign lands and cultures.

Shocking to me was the fact that, moved from primary school in Chalfont St. Giles to (private) prep school in Runfold, to grammar schools in Farnham and Ramsgate, and right through university I was exposed to single-sex education from the age of 7 to 23. Barfield, Farnham Grammar, Chatham House, St. Peter's College—learning devoid of females in any form, except one teacher, the sweet Miss Winnie Egan in Farnham.

As an adolescent student of the world, I was angry, alienated, frustrated, self-absorbed, and rather pathetic. Oh well, I moved on and grew out of it. I was caught between the innocent simplicity of childhood and the troubling complexity of adulthood, suspended in disbelief, trying to hold on to the carefree, while yearning to belong and take on responsibilities.

As Lord Byron sagely observed:

Then the season of youth and its vanities past,
For refuge we fly to the goblet at last;
There we find—do we not?—in the flow of the soul,
That truth, as of yore, is confined to the bowl.

Even in my teenage years, there stirred within me a yearning to escape, be a stage removed, head for the hills, hide out in nature, just as my father had felt impelled to leave the rat race of the London business world at the age of 40. While he threw it all in to dedicate his working life to providing convalescent holidays for underprivileged children, I was still making it up as I went, opting to log some miles and lap up travel and experience.

"Forest and rock know well how to be silent with you. Be like the tree again, the wide-branching tree that you love: calmly and attentively it leans out over the sea ... Flee, my friend, into your solitude and to where the raw, rough breeze blows! It is not your fate to be a fly-swat," whispered Nietzsche in *Thus Spake*

Zarathustra, so I bundled up my belongings and headed for the Alps.

On a heavenly bright morning, I hopped and skipped down the fast-melting, dripping slopes of Kranzberg with the frolic of a spring lamb. I gathered a sprig of purple heather and some dainty wild flowers as a romantic gift to this fantasy girl named Beate whom I had barely met, and clambered aboard the Enzian Express bound for München. In the twinkling of a mischievous eye, I was there, in the city, thrusting myself in her arms, and she in mine. There followed an exquisite day of strolling, laughter, Bierkeller merriness, lying in the spring sunshine of the vibrant university park; everybody looked so jolly, open and loose, as if each and every one had burrowed up from the underground darkness of hibernation to the glorious infancy of budding spring fever. There was conspiracy and lunacy in the air, and I was floating on whimsy. We made the plans of young lovers, impossible plans which would never materialize in a million moons, but, on such a blue moon day as this, I was not prepared to forfeit a clutch at stars, and we sat embraced, her pulsing body, her heaving breasts, her trembling hands, her quivering lips, touching, retreating, filling me with a flame which threatened to lick into open air. Such passionate desire assaulted me as never before, like forest fire attacking the tinder of dry wood. If ever I think of mad impulsiveness and living for a day, I think of Beate, the spring of young lust, and München. A lifetime flitted by my eyes in a day, an iridescent butterfly glowing orange and crimson in the charged amber sunlight. Before I knew it I was back on the train, my head in a dizzy whirl, my thoughts dazed, my body numb. I chuckled to myself, muttered exclamations of wonderment, felt jittery and quaking, and alternately trudged and floated back up the mountain. I had a pain in the pit of my stomach.

Again, Lord Byron captured the mood:

There is a pleasure in the pathless woods,
There is a rapture on the lonely shore,
There is society, where none intrudes,
By the deep sea, and music in its roar:
I love not man the less, but Nature more,
From these our interviews, in which I steal
From all I may be, or have been before,
To mingle with the Universe, and feel
What I can ne'er express, yet cannot all conceal.

Feeling a yearning to get out and explore the great outdoors, in my early twenties I put Oxford and Berlin behind me and threw myself into gardening full-time at the American Community School in Cobham, Surrey. I rented accommodation on a houseboat on a backwater of the Basingstoke Canal and cycled six miles each way to work each day, taking on the final mile a shortcut along the motorway. Thankfully, I was never stopped by the police. After years of travel by hitched rides, trains, buses and bikes, I took driving lessons and passed my test in Chertsey. This, my first and only full-time job in England, was very fulfilling. I loved working in the expansive bucolic gardens, in the fresh country air. Even now in later years, I dream of this time still. In the spring, nature unfolded gently with snowdrops and crocuses, daffodils and tulips. In summer, the rhododendron grove and azalea beds bloomed in a splash of vibrant colour, the grass grew lushly on the lawns and golf course and was neatly trimmed. I got to drive my first tractor. Herbaceous borders, sunken lavender gardens and beds of shrubs were weeded and spruced up. In the autumn, the leaves fell and were carted away. Come winter, it was time to cut back rampant growth, prune bushes, take out the dead wood. After the heavy frosts, blowing gales and very occasional snow, the birds, buds and insects heralded springtime once more.

Carl Jung's writings resonated with my love of the natural, as they emphasized the importance of balance and harmony. He cautioned that modern people rely too heavily on science and logic and would benefit from integrating spirituality and appreciation of unconscious realms. Jung's work on himself and his patients convinced him that life has a spiritual purpose beyond material goals. Our main task, he believed, is to discover and fulfill our deep innate potential, much as the acorn contains the potential to become the oak or the caterpillar to become the butterfly. Jung struck a chord with my own adolescent existence in *Memories, Dreams, Reflections*: "I saw myself as a rather disagreeable and moderately gifted young man with vaulting ambitions, an undisciplined temperament, and dubious manners, alternating between naïve enthusiasm and fits of childish disappointment, in his innermost essence a hermit and obscurantist."

I read Hermann Hesse's *Narziss and Goldmund*, *Steppenwolf*, *Siddhartha* and *The Glass Bead Game* (also known as *Magister Ludi*) which explore an individual's search for spirituality outside society. They introduced me to Eastern (especially Buddhist) thinking and captivated me, so it makes sense that these works set me off on my travels.

2

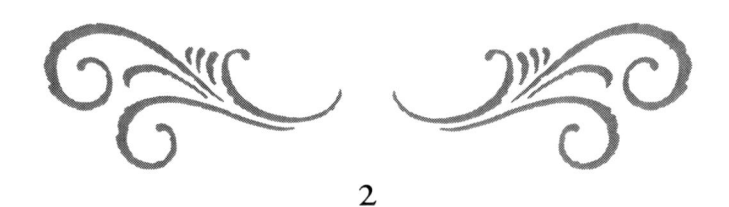

Migrating to the New World

Caminante, no hay camino, sino estelas en la mar ...

*Wanderer, your footsteps are
the road, and nothing more;
wanderer, there is no road,
the road is made by walking.
By walking one makes the road,
and upon glancing behind
one sees the path
that never will be trod again.
Wanderer, there is no road -
Only wakes upon the sea.*

(Antonio Machado, 1912, from "Proverbios y cantares" in *Campos de Castilla*)

After studies in Modern Languages (French and German) at Oxford and a couple of years of spinning my wheels gardening, my fate was decided in 1980 when Dad's younger brother Derek visited us in England. He had gone to Toronto, Canada, in 1950 to help his mother (my grandmother) relocate there and ended up immigrating himself. My grandmother had planned to return to England but died before I was born. Derek and his wife, Laura, persuaded me that a trip to Canada to work with my cousin Derek for a summer would be opportune. I took on part-time gardening jobs at the princely wage of £4 an hour in addition to my full-time work. Within a couple of months, I had enough to slap down £275 for a Wardair flight to Toronto. First, however, I had to go back again to Berlin for a week. It called to me. It was a muggy week, and my only real recollection is of a wild fling with the bubbly Ines, who was newly settling in the West from East Berlin and who had become a great friend of my sister Jill. We went swimming at the outdoor Insulaner pool, lolled in the sun and fooled around under the gaze of the moon. Mostly we just whispered, giggled and drooled. It was hot and steamy, lustful and lovely. We decided that I would move to Berlin and join her in her new flat after my ten-week trip to Canada. She would decorate it while I was away. However, something blocked the way of this plan, something that changed the course of my life entirely.

Once in a while, fateful encounters open up entire new vistas. In curiosity, I have always tried to follow my instincts and seek out new adventures. In following our hearts and minds, a beckoning destiny takes shape. As Antonio Machado wrote, we lead the way; there is no preordained path, and, as Sylvia Fraser wrote:

> Whatever has happened until now has had to happen;
> What is happening now is good;
> What will happen tomorrow is the best.

The summer in Ontario was fun, but I yearned to begin the next chapter in my life. I was leaving steady work and my native land behind. Up ahead was a new challenge, new vistas, horizons, prospects. I thought all these would meet me and Ines in Berlin, but, as it turned out, they came from a world away.

Very late on the last night of September 1981, I left my uncle, aunt and cousin after one last dinner out in downtown Toronto. The train bound for Vancouver, a new world to me some 4,500 kilometres distant and over 80 hours in travel time to the west, left just before midnight. The next day the train snaked ever so slowly around lakes and through gold and red forests as snow fell gently from the sky and settled softly over the landscape of northern Ontario. I struck up conversations with my fellow travellers as guitars were strummed. After a brief stretch of the legs in Winnipeg, we hopped back aboard to cross the wide-open prairies until the towers of Calgary popped above the horizon with the wall of the Rocky Mountains as a backdrop. Banff was delightful, especially the youth hostel, tucked away down the valley by the bubbling Bow River, and the mountainside hot springs.

Back on the train again, we sat a long time outside Lake Louise before pulling into the station. I caught sight of a woman on the platform preparing to board. Something about her turned my head. Before I knew it, she thankfully chose me to sit next to in the bar car. The conductor had suggested she go there while he arranged a seat for her. She revealed her name, Gundi.

We did the real stranger-on-a-train bit, blurting out our life stories and quite thinking that we would part the next day, never to meet again. Far from it. Five or six hours of conversation made it clear that we were already inseparable. I learned that Gundi's mother and father had decided to emigrate from Germany when she was just 11. They applied to move to Australia, New Zealand, South Africa and even Canada, where her father, Helmuth, had spent time (in Medicine Hat, Alberta) as a prisoner of war. They ended up in Chile, coming to love their adopted country. She lived in Santiago for around 20 years and married there, before emigrating once more (this time with then-husband Guillermo and their three daughters, Cristina, Claudia and Andrea), destined for Canada.

These many years later, Gundi, now divorced, was on a sales trip to Vancouver. She had no seat ticket, having boarded on the busy Thanksgiving weekend, but we told the conductor emphatically that—as we were getting on so famously—we needed to sit together. The conductor duly shook my snoring neighbour awake and moved him out. Gundi moved in. Before we knew it, hours and then a night of discovery had passed. She had grown on me, fast (and I on her, it seemed).

The next morning, the train was mercifully two hours late as it pulled into Vancouver. Gundi and I said our goodbyes, and I promised to call the number she had hastily scrawled. She didn't believe me, but I was true to my word. From outside Nanaimo on Vancouver Island, I caught her the evening before my flight back to London just as she was leaving to go out. We would meet for brunch at Emilio's, a bright Greek restaurant overlooking Granville Market by the water.

We had champagne and orange juice and eggs Benedict. The air was charged, and I insisted on paying the bill, leaving myself cleaned out of cash after a summer of work and travel. We then made a meal of our long, passionate farewell at Gundi's friend Linda's apartment. (We kicked Linda out for a couple of hours.) I spent the flight back to England consumed by how I would deal with Ines, who would be meeting me at the airport after a seven-hour wait following the arrival of her flight from Berlin. Worse still, a whole week with her lay ahead, a prospect that had been so beguiling just a few short days before. I dragged her to London for a job interview. Even before I met with her in Berlin in June, I had sent out numerous job applications, and now I desperately needed money. It was awful; poor, poor Ines. I called Gundi just to hear her voice and convince myself she was for real. I could not get her out of my head. I was cowardly to a fault, and Ines left without knowing what was really up. I could not bring myself to break up quite yet. My job interview for a large seismic-sounding company (whose main clients were Shell, Esso, Occidental and the like) in London was a success. I was hired and would be sent to work on a crew in the eastern Libyan desert starting in early December. Gundi and I had talked about meeting up in London at the end of December, as she would then be en route to Sri Lanka and Bali on a round-the-world trip. My work in Libya could not be postponed, so we gloomily realized that London was not a possibility. Gundi broke down and called back to suggest I come to Toronto for a few days before Libya. She offered to pay; I could pay her back later. So it was off to a discount travel agent's—fondly known in parlance as a bucket shop—just off Regent Street in Central London to purchase a plane ticket for a few days' hence. My poor mother couldn't believe it when I announced I was flying to Canada before Libya. What on earth for?

At the end of November 1981, I spent four blissful days and nights enveloped in Gundi's aura and embrace in intimacy never experienced before or since. The decision to come to Canada had been justified, and now it was crystal clear where my future lay. I just had my stint in Libya to get through, a minimum of two 10-week tours, with four weeks in between for us lovers to reconnect in person. It sounds straightforward enough, but it wasn't.

After a truck had driven over an anti-tank mine killing the driver, my main assignment in the Libyan desert a few hundred kilometres south of Benghazi was to oversee the safety of a mine-clearance operation. I took care not to reveal this to my nearest and dearest at the time.

My Libyan Desert Pass

In the Libyan desert, by midday, the winter temperature approaches 30 °C (85 °F); by mid-afternoon, 35–40 °C (over 100 °F). The broad expanses of sand and scrub stretching away to the horizon, be it of nearby ridges or the 50-mile distant skyline, give rein to a wealth of free-flowing reflections. It is wonderful to inhale air in surroundings completely uncluttered by the material comforts on which we ostensibly depend for meaning and security. To wander in the desert heat with only endless sand and endless sun entering my vision is liberating and exhilarating. My surroundings are bare, and I look at the naked form of my life, its subtle curves and sharp bumps hiding incomprehensible mysteries of what lies beyond the next rise, what lies in the middle distance ahead (as I can't quite make it out) and exactly where I am at this point. It is a purifying experience. Hindsight tends to distort and embellish, rendering shades of grey as vivid tableaux. However, moments of inspiration are worth waiting a hundred gloomy days for, and they fill the memory with real treasures.

I had to go out into the world to witness the hard life of basic subsistence and to observe the wonder of a pure desert sky at night. Only then could I come home and truly appreciate what I had to do with my life.

My bureaucratically delayed exit papers from Libya came through mid-February 1982, extending my first tour to 13 weeks. Back home in England I was able to telegraph Gundi that I would be arriving in Toronto in a few days' time. In these days before e-mail and mobile phones, the telegram was duly dispatched to the Masa Inn in Poppy's Lane in Kuta Beach, Bali, Indonesia, and I just hoped she would receive it. In Toronto I was met at the airport by my usually unflappable cousin Derek, who was flabbergasted to hear over beers that I had already paid one visit to Toronto since I had departed in September. Late for the eagerly anticipated flight's arrival, a lone woman walking away drew my eye way off in the distance. Was it her? It certainly was. We fell into each other's arms.

With the Libyan venture behind me, we spent several months purring through living together in Toronto. Then, after a transatlantic flight, Gundi and I were bound for the Far East on a luxuriant Singapore Airlines flight from London. This was true long haul. Having all my life never ventured outside Europe, here I was within a year travelling to North America, North Africa, and now Southeast Asia. Singapore was the ideal introduction, but its culture and steamy heat still slapped me.

The island of Bali was more intoxicatingly exotic, sensually appealing. So much so that I felt emboldened to propose marriage to Gundi at the most romantic spot I could conceive of: a charming restaurant overlooking a noisy fast-flowing river in the verdant jungle outside Ubud. The response I desired was not forthcoming. "Yeah, maybe; let's think about it," she replied.

Our three-month trip featured a month on magical mysterious Bali, a month travelling across busy yet beautiful Java and a couple of weeks of blissful idleness on the South Pacific–paradise of Pulau Tioman, a few hours by boat off the east coast of Malaysia. Travel can draw couples together or it can tear them apart as foibles rankle. We were drawn together enough to agree on a wedding date, October 1, 1983, later that year. It was up to me to apply for my immigration papers to Canada and to travel back to England to be interviewed at the Canadian Embassy in London. After endless weeks of waiting, my papers came through, and off I flew to embark on a new phase in life in Ontario. My immigration papers folded into my passport held an important proviso: "Must marry Gundi Viviani within 90 days of landing." The same document held an agreement signed by my future wife to sponsor me for 10 years; I had lucked out indeed! The customs and immigration officer in Toronto welcomed me in an Indian accent with words that are etched firmly in my memory: "Have a nice life in Canada."

> *The voice of beauty speaks softly: it steals into only the most awakened souls.* Nietzsche, *Thus Spake Zarathustra*

> *"I often lie awake at night from happiness, and all the time I think of our future life together. I have lived through much, and now I think I have found what is needed for happiness. A quiet secluded life in the country, with the possibility of being useful to people to whom it is easy to do good, and who are not accustomed to have it done to them; then work which one hopes may be of some use; then rest, nature, books, music, love for one's neighbour—such is my idea of happiness. And then, on the top of all that, you for a mate, and children*

perhaps—what more can the heart of man desire?" Leo Tolstoy, *Family Happiness*, 1859

So it was that, in my mid-twenties, I became an exile from my native Britain, settling in Canada just as my great-uncle, my uncle and my wife had all done before me. I will always retain a deep fondness and nostalgia for the "old country," especially the land itself. Love anchored me in a new life in a new land, provided me the soil, roots and sustenance to grow and mature. Having been planted on the island of Britain and grown as an infant sapling there, I became a transplant in the heart of the North American continent. Three years after immigrating, I was able to apply for Canadian citizenship. By answering correctly questions, such as, What is the capital of Quebec? and Who is the Prime Minister?, I became a Canadian, with the privilege of dual nationality. I was able to show my Canadian passport, much vaunted around the world, but I was also able, as a European of British nationality, to live and work anywhere within the European Union, and this privilege extended to my wife, too. Yet, I still wonder what might have become of my life had I not followed my intuition and taken that one romantic chance, made that one impulsive decision that changed my course completely. It could have been oh so different. Such is life.

Ever since meeting Gundi in one of those serendipitous, life-changing moments on the train in the Rocky Mountains of western Canada and moving to Ontario to share my life with her, we had lived in rented accommodation. Two freelance souls, our self-employed status meant one of us was always propping up the other, and times were sometimes tough. We wriggled our way through many a slim year, remaining true to our chosen vocations. Gundi went from fashion designer to clothes-shop assistant to flourishing glass artist. I went from landscape gardener to community college student to cartographer to map publisher. Our move from renting homes in the city of Toronto to owning a house and land in the country was achieved over a number of years. The list of rented homes is depressing in its length (and almost as long as the list of rented office spaces for my map business): Ontario Street, Munro Street, West Avenue, Glebeholme Avenue, Degrassi Street … We started on our exit route from the city by answering the call from an arresting ad in the paper. It seemed that I was driven by an unknown force to go out one bright September Saturday morning to pick up the *Toronto Star* at the corner of Degrassi and Dundas. I came home, opened the classifieds, and out popped, at the top of the list, "A unique opportunity." While Gundi was still sleeping, I called the number and arranged for a viewing that very day. "I know that place," Gundi said later. We drove out to the town of Dundas and, nestled above it, the village of Greensville. At the end of Stone Road, between Websters Falls and Tews Falls, on a precipice, beside the Bruce Trail, was 31 Fallsview Road, an absolute gem. Halley Schaub had grown up in the house but now lived in Ottawa, where her husband worked as a director at the National Research Centre, and so was letting the house. We supplied references and waited it out while Halley showed the house to others. I kept telling myself it had to be because it was meant to be. The house occupied a spectacular site overlooking the V-shaped wooded valley, with Hamilton Mountain capping the view at the far horizon. There was a magical aura about the place; despite being on the edge of a precipice, the house was solidly ensconced on a limestone escarpment, with a stream and cascading waterfall on each side embracing the site. It had been designed by a Californian architect as a ranch-style house with a flat roof sitting amid enormous oak and maple trees. It had been a very modern design when built in the late 1950s and exuded a strong presence.

We got it. We were pinching ourselves for our good fortune most of the time we lived there, over four years. It was a special time in our lives, and we look back on it now with nostalgia. I won't forget being snowed in one winter; we went for a walk in snow up to our thighs in places and arrived home spent. We were enraptured by both waterfalls, the hike to the peak, and the beauty of the valley trail winding back up beside the coiling creek toward the house. It felt like a world apart. For a while I commuted first into Mississauga and then Oakville until my map business partner, Arlene, made things much simpler for herself, and for me, by moving to Dundas, giving me a five-minute drive to work. Because of the steepness of the hill, I cycled to work on only two occasions, I believe. When Halley decided to sell, Gundi and I agonized over whether to buy the house. The appraisal came in and we made an offer well below Halley's evaluation, which was inflated by her attachment to her childhood home. Our offer was seen as derisory and we were rebuffed, so we upped sticks once more, landing on our feet again on the Niagara Escarpment 10 miles or so east on Mountainbrow Road, Waterdown.

Here we took in, then promptly lost, our first little puppy, Solo. He was quite a handful and got away from me, to encounter a pickup truck on the road. I buried him in a shallow grave back in the woods; there is only a thin layer of humus on top of the limestone. I went to visit him tearfully for a few days, then decided it was time for a last goodbye, a final apology. A soft snow was falling and the woods were all white. As I turned away from him, I looked up to see a large buck deer looking me straight in the eye just 50 feet or so away. As I moved, the deer bounded off, and Solo's spirit was released. Coyotes cleaned off his bones in the days to come. We almost instantly replaced him with Gato, who just showed up one day in late winter. Gundi found him whimpering behind her stack of glass beside the house, brought him indoors and plonked him on my lap. A kitten at the time, he took a good look around and decided this was his new home. We posted a notice, "Grey cat found," and were joyous after two days elapsed and we got to keep him. Up next was Negra, the last kitten Gundi's youngest daughter, Andrea, was finding a home for after her cat Lucky had produced her litter. Negra was a small, shy black cat that eluded prospective new owners. And this sweet girl—still our *negrita*—remains a delight to us both.

Gundi and Peter, married two years

3

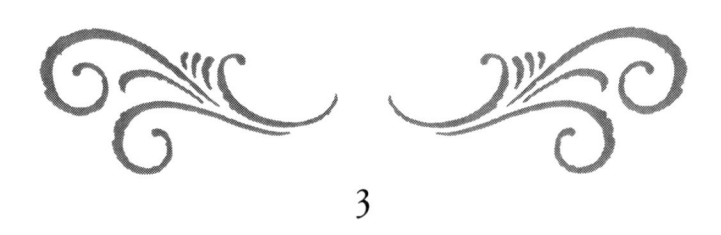

A Sense of Arrival

The years had whizzed by. Already married for sixteen years, and with me in my early forties, our first attempt at owning a house had made us realize that it was high time for a new challenge, a sea change for us both, a midlife move to a whole new lifestyle.

Neither of our cats was happy at our move into home ownership. This was the big one. Our nine lives as renters were up. Those pesky landlords had finally driven us out of leases and monthly rental payments. They had each either sold up or moved back in. So began the hunt for property and application for mortgages for a pair of self-employed creatives. We had always loved camping and cottaging in what is known simply as the County—Prince Edward County, that is, on the Bay of Quinte. Our trips had begun at Salmon Point, then we graduated to South Bay, and always en route, we drove past the appealing sign for Shelter Valley Road along Highway 401. Peering down from the highway along this treed road winding up into the hills, it called to us. On one slow drive back home from the County to the city, we heeded the call and drove into a wonderful up-and-down landscape which seemed almost Alpine with its rolling meadows and quaint wooden homes, compared to the regular flat grid of southern Ontario.

We decided to cast our net and hooked up with a real estate agent whose listings reflected our desires, such as we understood them: a house with character, off the main roads, with a little bit of land; four or five acres seemed plenty. Barry came up with a host of potentials for our first foray. At the end of our first viewing day, we looked back at a series of properties which didn't quite do it for us and set off for an overnight stay in Campbellford, where we would view one more place with another agent the next morning. As we drove east, the late afternoon sun brought into focus a lovely pastoral scene of large round bales and their shadows and a curving, shorn, golden hillside.

The view that sold us

Gundi said we had just passed a sign that lay almost in the ditch, so we turned back. It read "House and 55 acres." Oh boy, there was a house back there along that lane, tucked behind the hill! At the peak of the last steep hill, we were able to pick out the peak of the roof set way, way back from the road. Giddy with excitement, we called Barry from Campbellford and asked why he hadn't sent us this listing. Apparently he had. We had overlooked it because of the poor photograph of the back of the house, which had made it look so dark and blockish on a fax, and because the address was on a main road.

The next morning we met Barry at the road. There was nobody home. As we were leaving, the owners pulled up but said they weren't ready to show the house. Paul and Marie Von Baich reluctantly agreed to allow us poor folk (who had come so far) to view the house in an hour's time, giving them time to rearrange the clutter. In the meantime we could explore the land. Barry and I drove the 1,200 feet of laneway to the house; Gundi was determined to approach on foot, breathing in the fresh summer country air and soaking up the aura. By the time she met me at the house, we were both convinced that this was the place for us. "Let's hope the inside is okay," we said. The house was so filled with papers and piles of stuff and masked behind heavy drapes that it was hard to get a sense of the dimensions, shape and flow. Our disorientation was increased by the unusual way that each room on all three levels fed off the central chimney, which was on a diagonal to the rectangular frame of the building. Paul had designed the house and had it built. He did everything right: he had tucked it into the back of a north-facing hill; set it back from the road to look out over fields and rolling hills, with different views in all directions; planted lots of pines and poplars for shade and wind protection; faced the house due south to maximize use of passive-solar heat. His genius extended to building in an extra-thick layer of insulation to buffet the building from the prevailing westerly winds that seasonally blew strong and from the biting winter cold which got down to minus 30–35 ºC (minus 20–30 ºF). He said his initial goal was to be able to heat the house with a candle!

A week later, the place was ours; we owned our first house (and 55 acres)! I can't pretend it was easy for two self-employed souls to be approved a mortgage. Negotiating with three banks, it was nip and tuck, and we lied about our income and about the house's sole source of heat being a wood-burning stove, which had threatened to be a deal breaker for the mortgage insurance. Paul and Marie were eager to sell, and we agreed on a price at the second signing back. We were elated, yet apprehensive.

After packing up and moving two businesses and a household, along with the endless documentation involved with buying our first house, we collapsed into our new home in a daze. Alive enough to stare out in wonder at our new country home and land, we couldn't believe our luck (and good taste!). In late October, the leaves on the poplars were few, and they shivered nervously at the prospect of the coming cold. One by one they gave up and flew down to earth. The hum of life quieted to a whimper, and yellow turned to brown. We'd missed the fall colours, and just the pines stood resolute all around the house. The view south opened up, and the fields paraded. Finally the creek showed its shy smile, marsh cheeks wafting in the wind.

The house was a mess, with pieces of wood everywhere and boxes of curios dotting the floor and closets. We set about unpacking things with a vengeance, Gundi the artful queen of inspired placement. Within days, our new home took shape and evolved in a sort of serendipitous way. The kitchen remained an open, effortlessly functional country kitchen with utensils out in sight. Feasts for dinners began immediately; there were no canned, frozen or prepackaged meals for us. The plentiful cupboards and closets offered ample space for parking things. Gundi's glass and my maps and satellite images packaged by the hundreds found their home down in the walkout basement in the designated glass studio and map room.

And then that was it; there we were, waiting for the world to catch up to us. The mail took a few weeks, as did the business telephone installation. Running two new lines back from the road and hooking them up tried my patience and the rural resources of Bell Canada. If only we had had other options. In my haste, I had given friends and family an incomplete change of address, so County Road became our new street name, though even this often got corrupted to Country Road. Eventually, we dropped the security blanket of a street number and settled on just the rural route number, or sometimes even just the postal code. It amazed us how the local post office traced us easily that way from day one, and the thrill of having all mail delivered to our roadside box was great. So began the daily trip to the road to receive word from the outside world. The trip was a drive until Gundi's grandson Skye reminded me that a bike would be the better choice (he sent me a postcard asking if I rode out to pick it up). But then winter set in, and the ride became a windy jog or, more usually, a drive combined with a trip to homely Warkworth or riverside Campbellford, or, further afield, the bank, restaurants and big shopping in Cobourg or Peterborough.

Andrea and her sons, Skye and Lake, came to stay, and instead of the few hours' visit we had been accustomed to, we were treated to a visit of a few days. They set to work constructing a poplar lookout and making valued suggestions. We set about adding some colour to our white interior—ocean blue living room, desert yellow office for me, then the wildly ambitious wild rose bedroom, which we still coo at. The first coat looked horrifically fleshy, the second more rosy, the third rich and just right, after a week or two of acclimatization. The white chimney became first golden brown and then was enhanced by a green patina; then we forgot about it, so I imagine it's all right.

With the cold came the first delivery of wood from Carman Atkinson, neighbour and previous owner of our property. It wasn't a great first batch; we contended with lots of smoke and green fires. Local contractor Larry Vanslyke spent a couple of hours hacking away at the build-up of creosote in both chimneys and cleaning them out to a perfect rectangle. He reckoned they hadn't been cleaned for a few years. Slowly we got the hang of ordering, chopping, stacking, drying, and burning the wood, and before long, fragrant full-flame fires were lighting up our evenings and keeping the chill off at night. The house is so well insulated, we're still amazed. Even at the low winter temperatures, on sunny days, we rarely light the woodstove before the sun goes down. Never have we been so toasty at home in winter at such cold temperatures. And, by the end of our first full winter, we had burned just over two bush-cords of mixed hardwood, for a total heating bill of $300. This represented a savings for us of over $1,000! When we went away for the weekend a couple of times, we turned on electric space heaters to keep the edge off, and the house was fine. It took a couple of days to get the temperature back to normal, but that was to be expected.

Our first winter was mild. There were no huge blockbuster snowstorms; the worst we got were two- to three-inch falls for a week or two in February, followed by six inches or so. So the biggest accumulation was around a foot, blowing to more in drifts. But the anticipated blowing-in of the sloping driveway never really happened. Neighbour Joe blew out the laneway twice in a week and that was it. The cost each time was just $12, or a dollar a minute on Joe's scale. Of course, the four-wheel drive of our Pathfinder, "Beast," was invaluable, its only downside being the gouging of deep ruts during the spring melt, which came fast in March, and the lane became a morass. I dug ditches to drain off the water in gushing courses, but the mud sat there for a couple of weeks, rutted further by any four-wheeled traffic. And then it dried up. I filled in the ruts by spadework, ran the Beast up and down it a few times, and there we had it, a working laneway.

However, we really would need ample infusions of gravel in the hollows to escape the worst of it.

That winter was highlighted by some memorable discoveries. Our magical cedar introduced herself early, and Gundi was especially enraptured. She was majestic and huge (the cedar, not Gundi), pointing heavenward in seven or eight stooping, arching, then soaring stems. The marsh and creek became accessible only when we discovered the tractorway to it on the east side. At that point the creek looked like a running stream rather than the number of shallow channels that it was at the culverted west of our property. The marsh was broad where it crossed our land, but we could only really get at it when the creek was truly frozen over. This didn't happen until about February; even then, there were open stretches showing signs of beavers and deer-foraging. On a crisp, bright, blue-skied February day following a fresh snowfall, we got to explore the creek by walking along it. It felt as if we were in virgin territory, divorced momentarily from humanity, with just wolf tracks ahead of us on the glistening white surface. We meandered around the bends before we arrived at an open stretch dotted with deer tracks and we clambered up the hillside back home. The air was still and bracing. Often, we would hike up to the top of the hill, to the top of our world. The sweeping view was always changing, depending on the season and the weather. In winter, the winds could be biting, but the reward was a real uplifting of spirits. We saw in the year 2000 with just the two of us and a bottle of bubbly, the fireworks in Roseneath, Hastings, even Cobourg flickering in the cloudy sky at the passing of midnight. Otherwise, one car passed in an hour on our lonely County Road, and we heard just the whistling of the wind on a mild night.

4

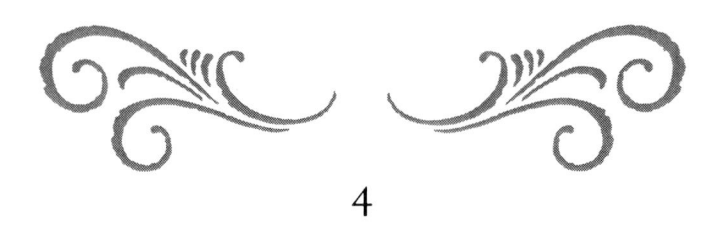

Into a New Millennium

2000

> *I went to the woods because I wished to live deliberately, to front only the essential facts of life. And see if I could not learn what it had to teach, and not, when I came to die, discover that I had not lived.* (Henry David Thoreau.)

I went to the land and the hills for the same reason.

On my return from a business trip in February, a curious event occurred. I woke up early in the morning to the sound of a cat racing from room to room. I got up in the half dark just as Negra, still a kitten really, knocked over glass bottles lined up in the guest-room window and literally climb the walls in a frenzy. I grabbed her, and she sank both sets of claws deep into my hands. Blood dripping over the floors, I bandaged them up and observed this little black cat cowering under the corner of the bed. A couple of hours later she came downstairs, but we kept our distance, still wondering what was up. Then came the sounds of a cat fight in the guest room. We went up to discover that our other cat, Gato, had penned an unknown item under the bed. We lifted the covers to discover ... a black cat! Negra was downstairs. Who was this? Gloved, this time, Gundi lifted out this Negra look-alike. We inspected her carefully and then tossed her out the door. Then my hands swelled up. I called the hospital and the nurse advised me to go to emergency immediately. We began to really question which cat had clawed me. If it hadn't been Negra, we hadn't a clue who this other cat was. I got tetanus shots and I was advised to find the cat to avoid rabies shots, given the risk it might have been a wild cat. So here was a chance to get out and meet the neighbours.

I began with Greg and Teresa who I had never met and who lived in the white house out our laneway and over on the other side of the main road. They had a cat, but not a black one. Ambrose and Joanne in the farmhouse up the hill had many cats, including barn cats, a black one among them, but not the right cat. Carman and Keitha beyond them had had the brutal old-fashioned long-syringe rabies shots but did not presently have a black cat. Joe said that if he ever saw a black cat on his property, he would shoot it (just as he shot on sight any raccoon, skunk, groundhog, rabbit, or deer). Slobo, in the house directly opposite our entrance from the road, had a number of Rottweilers that yelped loudly for much of the day as they were cruelly tethered on short leashes to nasty-looking kennels. He was said to have a black cat but didn't really want to discuss it with us and never answered the door when we dropped by to see him. This left us with his next-door neighbour Amy, who we knew bred Bouvier dogs, but she seemed suspicious of answering questions about her black cat, who, of course, wouldn't scratch or bite anybody! After a chat on the phone, she invited me to visit, and I met her and her four kids, all very sweet, especially the oldest girl, Charmaine, who listened all ears, just as our grandson Skye did. Must be the home-schooling. Sure enough, a placid little black pussycat that Amy assured me had had her shots was the creature I was looking for. She might have been the cat that scratched me, but I tend to think it must have been Negra who had been spooked by having a strange black cat come into her house. Since it was not a feral cat that had been responsible, I was able to call the concerned Regional Medical Officer of Health back to reassure him that I would not be the first human fatality from rabies in Ontario for 40 years. His description of how the rabies virus takes up to six months to travel from the veins to the brain (by which time it will always be fatal) had spooked me, though.

April was a month of thwarted anticipation. Cold temperatures dragged on, we tired of winter and just wanted to get out and grow things. Jamie helped me to gather two truckloads of tires, plastic and junk all half buried in the garden. It was off to the dump with it all, and good riddance. We then started clearing the old vegetable garden and digging the soil over; it was good soil. In moving to the country I had no inkling that this very soil would one day soon make me a livelihood, would transform my life, my mental well-being and my physical health.

Carman had in recent years grown turnips and potatoes on the side of the hill along the driveway. There must have been good soil there too, I assumed, as the produce tasted wonderful. Carman had already mulched the area with straw, so I set about digging 20 rows, each 20 feet long, in preparation for the planting of several hundred garlic bulbs, my precious purchase from Portuguese Mary in Waterdown, where we had moved from. It was reputed to be great garlic! I planted them sometime in late April, I believe. Not ideal planting time, I know, so I was thrilled to see the shoots appear soon after, but I was not so tickled to see the weeds fill in at an alarming rate, and continuing to do so all summer. In May, in went new, red and white potatoes and Spanish and white onions.

We dug wooden planks in around what would become

Gundi's vegetable garden and prepared the ground for the seeding of peas, radishes, mixed salad greens, lettuce, and carrots and the planting of kohlrabi, cardoons, tomatoes, basil, green peppers and hot peppers. All of it was prolific and beautifully rich in flavour, including the carrots, which made a late spurt.

Next up were the herbs. Over the winter, I had purchased organic seeds from nearby Richter's, including basil, dill, rosemary, lavender, parsley and cilantro. With Gundi getting straight into seeding the parsley, cilantro, basil and dill like wildfire, I ended up seeding just the lavender and rosemary (both slow and difficult, yet valuable) indoors in trays. Chard, arugula and rapini were planted directly outdoors in hastily dug beds in the field just below Gundi's patch. Neighbour Joe labelled the soil stony and sandy, "mean ground," as he called it. However, with gradual enhancement with mulch and compost over the years, this glacial till became perfect loamy soil for growing greens.

In March, friends Lucy and Roy had gone on a memorable trip to Provence and Corsica, and Lucy came back with the suggestion that I grow lavender, fields of it. Brilliant! I set to research, and sure enough, it was suitable for our zone 5 climate. The English Hidcote and Munstead varieties were more hardy than the Provençal, but even the last stood a chance of surviving the winter if sufficiently protected with mulch. Off we went to Richter's, where I purchased several flats of English and French lavenders to see how these would fare. I also purchased a flat of tarragon. Gundi came back with her regular $50 to $100 worth of varied goodies, some unpronounceable. Into the mean ground went the lavender, and for weeks it looked very cold and uncomfortable.

Spring came and went with whiffs of caragana and honeysuckle by the house, lilacs and apple blossom down the laneway and the heavenly scent of flowering honey locusts outside the kitchen window. The air is always so fresh here, the wind often invigorating, but the smells of fresh earth and blooms at springtime must eclipse all others, except maybe the first hay cutting of the year.

If life emits a fragrance like flowers and sweet herbs ... that is your success. (Henry David Thoreau)

We were treated in late May to lunch at Ambrose and Joann's at the top of the hill to the west. We had a gut-busting meal followed by the royal tour of the 600-acre family estate, now divided between two sons. Theirs were modern intensive agricultural concerns with all the big toys required to keep them essentially one-man operations. Ploughs had been discarded for this insane new world of no-till farming, Roundup application in the fall followed by Roundup Ready seeding in the spring. What was this really doing to our food in the way of trickle-down residuals? I redoubled my resolve to build a truly organic approach to cultivating the land, whatever form that took in the years to come. Industrial-scale crop yields may have been sizeable and largely weed-free, and the planting and harvesting may have been a piece of cake for one man and his two sons, but these methods compromised the long-term health of the soil. It used to take a platoon and probably weeks to do the same work. Ambrose himself was of the generation that had cleared these fields in the first place, rock by rock, with pure brute strength. And the poison ivy was apparently no picnic either. Now, with understandable pride, he surveyed the fruits of his own and others' toil: the enormous fields, hundreds of acres of them, progressively denuded of dividing treelines, produced corn, soybeans, grain for commodity markets and alfalfa hay for livestock feed. It was hard work still, although sometimes the price was attractive, and there was always the dairy quota they could depend on through the

Milk Marketing Board. These hardened farmers had to be pretty dedicated to stick to it when the elements conjured up their potion of often untimely rains, snows, blizzards, freezing rains, droughts, cold snaps, heat waves. And it always had to get dark before the day's work was truly done.

Ambrose, in his eighties, mocked his cousin Carman for his forays into growing all manner of crops organically, including sweet corn, blueberries, turnips and potatoes. Apparently Carman was so kind-hearted that he was forever helping others, so much so that he was dismissed by some as a dabbler and not a true farmer. However, in his sunset years, Ambrose had wisdom enough to travel several miles on his Gator golf-cart-like conveyance (purchased after his driver's license was taken away) to get his free-range eggs. He would often come over our fields, intrigued by all the different herbs and vegetables here, and marvel at the wild bees on the fragrant flowering buckwheat and red clover. He loved to buy our garlic, which he ate raw with his morning porridge, and always insisted on paying for it though he wouldn't take a penny from me for the plum and raspberry suckers and strawberry plants he graciously offered up. We had always wondered about the beautiful tree at the fenceline that always caught the setting sun. "That's a balm o' Gilead," Ambrose declared with authority.

All summer, our first one here in the hills, we feasted on the garden's fresh bounty—various mixed salad greens, lettuce, parsley and endless dill, which punctuated the garden in tall sprigs. The English lavenders grew shyly, but the Provençal bushed out quite nicely. I mowed between the rows and weeded occasionally. The garlic required ample attention; on planting in early spring, I had not anticipated the knots of roots from the straw filling in so rampantly, along with other weeds too. I weeded the beds through the summer, determined to give them their best opportunity to show what they could do. Next door neighbour Len had kindly offered me use of his rototiller, and I had taken him up on it and tilled up the hillside patch next to the garlic. But where Carman had put straw down, it was too thick for tilling. Into the tilled patch I put a few scant rows of new and red potatoes, and onions, and Gundi planted leeks, Brussels sprouts, a few tomatoes and broad beans. This patch grew in with weeds, and the potatoes were infested with potato bugs; however, they grew, and we savoured them.

Summer came in with fairly regular downpours. This played in our favour since I had no means to water the plants on this hillside. The garlic thrived, growing tall, and we plucked its scapes as they formed. Then came the glorious day in early August when Andrea and her little ones chanced to be here for a few days. We dug up the first garlic bulb, and Andrea deemed it prime time to pick the rest before they turned mouldy. So the harvest began, with Skye, Lake, toddler Poppy, Andrea and Gundi all helping to dig, pile up the barrow and baskets and then set the bulbs out in the sun to dry. We were blessed with several days of sun and breeze, ideal conditions for drying. Then we knocked off the dirt, braided some prime specimens and laid the entire harvest out in the shed. And what a harvest it was. We had plump, juicy bulbs of which I was truly proud.

Gundi is a wonderful artist, naturally talented, boundlessly creative, eminently resourceful and infinitely patient. Her artistic vocation had begun with fashion design training at Sheridan College in Oakville before we met. She then set up in business as Gundi Design Workshop and specialized in dramatic leather and suede coats and jackets, which she sold successfully for many years to clothing stores in Toronto. Following a visit to Berlin and a seminal visit to the grand Pergamon Museum with its Greek installations, she came home inspired to work at creating mosaics. She chose glass as her medium, and within a few short years, she was creating unique stacked-glass sculptures which kept getting bigger and better and bolder. She had found her niche at the Buyers Market of American Craft in Philadelphia, a show held twice a year at which she sold her creations to high-end galleries across the United States. In 2000, she was presented an award from *Niche* magazine for Best Flat Glass in North America.

Now, in August, Gundi was fiendishly busy keeping up with orders for her glass sculptures. In planning her schedule in February, she hadn't anticipated so many re-orders in the summer. Her success was a real boon; we had never been able to save as she did at this point. She had already opted to take a sabbatical for the summer Philadelphia trade show, and this proved to be wise; she was busier than she wanted to be for a second year now. It was going to be interesting to see if we could gauge her order schedule right for her next year, and she was already campaigning for more holiday time. We hadn't been away for a couple of years, so we were gearing up.

In the meantime, it was renovation time. The dismal, cramped bathroom and separate toilet were at the top of our list for a major overhaul. In June, local contractor Larry began tearing out walls and opening up the bathroom, toilet and bedroom walk-in closet. In went a new window on the west of the house; in went new pipes and plumbing and off we went to buy sink, toilet, shower stall, floor tiles, doors, paint and my prized, massive $300 bath tub. Mostly fittings came from a big box store. We had cast around for local suppliers but ended up at a one-stop shop for choice and economy. And what a transformation. Larry's brother-in-law, Al, installed the dry-wall, and I laid the floor and painted the walls, and suddenly we had a sparkling new bathroom.

Next up we decided we had to drill a new well to improve water volume. We had been fortunate that with the plentiful rains, our existing shallow dug well had to date offered up just enough water to get by, but we constantly had to be very frugal with bathing, flushing the toilets and washing clothes. The big drilling rig, operated by crusty old Don, arrived and set to bore. He hit hard rock or a thick layer of shale at around a hundred feet down and had to extract all that depth of pipe that he had already lain because of this. So down they went again with a wider drill bit, and three weeks later, we hit heavenly water, lots of it, at 153 feet. Then the connection to the house went in; luckily Herb Lang was able to hook up to the well and avoid costly trenching to the house. It was expensive enough, though, at $29 per foot and almost $3,000 for the hook-up, filter cap and submersible pump. The fun part of this exercise for me had been dowsing for the well location with Herb, who used a divining rod. He found the good spot straight away, with the rod showing a strong east-to-west and north-to-south intersection. I was thrilled to get identical results, so that's where we dug. We had a few days of doubt as we drew up very metallic, cloudy water, but then we heeded Herb's advice that we thoroughly flush out the pipes. After months of sparing every drop of water, old habits died hard. Plentiful, pure water from deep in the earth was such a precious resource. Later, I discovered an old hand pump lying in the grass beside the well, so we may at some point connect this up, and have a back-up manual system.

2001

Our second winter was a nice white one, with snow on the ground almost constantly from the beginning of December 2000 to the end of March 2001. Gundi showed her glass sculptures in Philadelphia, with sales just about doubling over last year's show! This would lead to a frantically busy summer for her. My own map-business commitments also meant we had to put off our two-week holiday in Mexico until the end of April. Then it was back home to springtime in full tilt and the frenzy of preparing the garden for rows of herbs. I decided to buy culinary herbs in plug trays that hold over a hundred single seedlings since these were economical yet reliable. So, it was off to Richter's for what would be my annual plant purchase for a number of years. I drove home with the heavenly fragrance of spearmint, lemon balm, English lavender, rosemary, Greek oregano, sage, thyme, bergamot and double chamomile filling the car. In the seedlings went at the beginning of June. Their first summer turned out to be a hot, dry one with no rain for about six weeks, from the end of June to mid-August. They received many, many drinks from the watering can, and they all survived and ultimately thrived.

What a summer our second year conjured up! Ambrose said he'd been around these parts for 80 summers, but he'd never known one this dry and hot. For six weeks starting about at the end of May, there was barely a drop of rain, and certainly not enough to slake the thirst of needy plants. The poor old potatoes on the laneway hillside seemed to cope the worst, shrivelling up into brown droops and yielding only a tiny handful of fruits each. Everything that went unwatered over there, including my treasured garlic as well as onions, responded with puny harvests. The garlic looked so poorly that I pulled it all in one fell swoop at the beginning of August, although it had only been planted in spring. The result was a lot of immature bulbs with unformed cloves, a smattering of ripe but small bulbs, and a lot of useless tiny ones. After also losing a lot to mould over the winter in the cold room, stocks for the farmers market were low. However, I had committed myself to three months of selling at my first farmers market, in nearby Campbellford, from August to October. It turned into a pleasant enough experience. The herbs seemed impervious to the drought, though I had kept them kicking with my watering. So off I went, somewhat tentatively, early on Saturday mornings to show my bunches of basil, mints, cilantro, chives; pots of rosemary, sage, thyme, lemon balm and spearmint; garlic plants and braids; and then sundry dried herbs in small glass jars. French lavender was top in this category. The lavender we had planted in our first summer now bushed out and flowered sumptuously.

Provençal lavender

The extended hot, dry weeks of June and July were a boon to the French lavender especially. My favourite task of this period was snipping and bunching the long stems, with their scent of camphor, and hanging them in the porch to dry the flower heads. Two weeks later, I rubbed the flowers from the stems into fragrant piles, bottled them and took them to market to waft under customers' noses. The lemon balm, Greek oregano and double chamomile all spread themselves out. The garden sage grew strong and proud into full, pungent bushes. The spearmint started well, then stuttered, all the while spreading its fiendish sucker roots underground. The rosemary and new lavender seedlings both looked very content with life and bushed up promisingly. The

English thyme took its time but survived with vigour. Just the bergamot failed to thrive, becoming mildewed and straggly. All in all, a successful first season for the Hills Herbs. Oh, yes, mustn't forget "and Flowers": sunflowers were the big hit. Although two of the six exotic varieties we had planted didn't peep above the surface, those that did performed rather well, especially the solid endurance and the proud Russian mammoth varieties, which provided enough seed for an army. Sunflowers were tremendously popular in September at the market, and I sold all that I took each of four weeks. I determined to grow more next year and planned to branch out into other types of cut flowers. The problem was the short growing season, of course. Without a greenhouse to bring seedlings on in early spring, I was forced to choose flowers whose seeds could be planted directly without transplanting. This limited my options, but I made do. I grew bit by bit and learned as I went. The statice, scabious and helichrysum didn't come on through the dry, hot spell, but then it was extremely dry (for six long weeks) and extremely hot (over 35 ºC, or around 100 ºF, for over a week in August). The nigella made a late showing, and I liked the pretty pods and the preceding Persian jewels flowers in their mixed colours. I took to taking mixed herb gardens in plastic containers to market and sold quite a few, to my surprise, with the combinations of rosemary, sage and thyme, and spearmint, lemon balm and oregano doing well.

In summer, insects were everywhere; the air was swarming and oppressive in its fullness. Crickets and cicadas sizzled. The plants enjoyed their growth spurt. Animals were out gorging on the plenty all around. Summer's languid heat made us strip down to bare essentials in movement as well as in dress. It was hard to keep up with nature's profligacy; we kept cutting back the grass, chopping back the weeds, until fall, when we sat back and gaped at the astounding colours of the leaves and waited for winter to call us indoors to charge our batteries for the onslaught of the next outdoor season.

At the end of the growing season, it was time to experiment with drying the sage, oregano, mint, lemon balm, rosemary, thyme and chamomile flowers. My favourites were the rosemary, balm and mint, but I was very pleased with the strength of all of them. I made a very soothing digestive tea blend from the dried bergamot, lemon balm and spearmint.

> *Out of the flux of today with billions fleeing into the famine of urbanization, the small farmer can rise again with a bio-plan in hand. A small farmer carries a vocation in his heart. It is possibly the most important vocation on the planet. It is the gift to grow. It is the knowledge and wisdom to take the seed from youth to adolescence through to maturity.*

(Diana Beresford-Kroeger, *The Global Forest*)

Harry, fellow farmer at the market, urged me to go for organic certification, suggesting that it was necessary to sell to certain commercial buyers. So I filled out the comprehensive forms from OCPP and sent in my $200 in November, hoping that I might be able to label all my produce "verified organic" in time for the next season. At this same time I answered the battle call to defend our local fields from the dreaded sewage sludge from Toronto, with my aim to help create a safe community rather than just an organic corner of it. So much damage had already been done to local land by the application over many years of chemical and toxic fertilizers, pesticides, herbicides, fungicides, antibiotics, liquid manures and livestock feed, which have all been washed into watersheds, wells, aquifers and eventually our common water supply. Toxins were already pervasive in the country air that we breathed, especially at times when we were downwind of spraying operations. Now the threat of heavy metals and toxins from the mega-city's household, institutional and industrial wastes being fobbed off on our fields, simply because it was the cheapest way to dispose of it, was appalling. What the authorities wouldn't acknowledge is that they didn't fully understand the long-term consequences of their actions, but then neither did they care because they wouldn't be around in thirty years to have to deal with the irreparable damage to our water supply, the pollution and degradation of the air or the poor health of our children. How short-sighted our society has become in the shameless pursuit of money.

We had been transplants in the countryside for two years now. It felt refreshingly longer than that, and we were now fully attuned to the rewards and the challenges. The country represented a simpler lifestyle, which we had pursued to escape or minimize the trappings of material consumption, of "getting ahead." We really didn't want to get ahead of anyone; instead we sought to get among like-minded people, even kindred souls. And it happened. We found a lovely mix of creative, contented, honest souls using their positive energies to express themselves in their professions, pastimes, vocations and interests. We had settled into a routine of a busy work life with social outings on the weekends. New friends all had wonderful houses and properties with charm and character. They were all tucked away in their homes in the hills, working honestly to live well.

We were constantly rewarded in our pursuit of the good life by an almost pristine beauty in our surroundings. I found this beauty notably stark when winter came upon us. We were delivered an amazing November of mostly bright, clear skies and unseasonably mild temperatures. Then, overnight, came a sharp jolt of cold with a white blanket of heavy frost and a chilly, still bright day. Suddenly, the rolling hills and woodlands looked stiff and solitary and the prospect of being out there in wide-open nature under cover of darkness a daunting prospect, with nothing as accompaniment but a crackle of wild animal movements or the howling of packs of coyotes or the smell of their wildness.

2002

Just before garlic-planting time in 2001, I had paid a visit to the Fish Lake Garlic Man, Ted Maczka, who lived tucked away on a back road of Prince Edward County. It was a Sunday morning, and having negotiated my way through the assorted clutter of his garden path, I met Ted eager to talk garlic and suck on raw cloves of it.

Ted Maczka, The Fish Lake Garlic Man. Photo by L. Matin

His 15 or so raised beds of well-built-up organic soil, gently improved with fertility every growing season over probably 20 years, were primed for their next impregnation with seed. He showed me proudly into his Aladdin's Cave, a padlocked school bus containing his museum collection of garlic specimens, his meticulous records of experimentations and findings and his treasured display of newspaper articles extolling the health virtues of garlic and its suitability for growing in Ontario. He kept up his eternal mischief in battling the authorities and the powers that be. He told me that, on retiring from his factory work way back when, he had asked the provincial agriculture experts about growing garlic, and they had laughed him off, telling him that conditions in Ontario were not conducive to garlic-growing. Nothing could be further from the truth, as we all now know. We cut some garlic, and popped two of Ted's favourite pungent garlics into my mouth, and their flavour invaded my palate and danced up my nostrils on this still young morning. His price for garlic bulbs was $8 per pound, so I decided on a few pounds each of Rocambole and Red Russian, the only real difference being the number of cloves each bulb produced—six to eight for Rocambole, just four for Red Russian. Intrigued by Ted's success, I asked where most of his business came from. Surprisingly, it was not from farmers markets or annual local garlic festivals but mail order (to places around the world) through word of garlic mouth. I thought, *Hmm, nice way to do business.* I envisaged selling garlic and herbal products (dried herbs, teas, oils, vinegars, tinctures, creams, ointments, balms) through a Web site. To this day, the prospect of planting a couple of acres of hard-neck garlic, mulching it for the winter, watching it grow to maturity, harvesting and drying it, then selling it all at full market price is immensely appealing.

> *Other than sex, for which it is a mythic metaphor, no act is as intimate as planting a seed. Watching something infinitely*

fragile sprout in warm, fertile earth and nursing it along to the point where it can survive and grow strong is practically definitive of what it is to be human. (Christina Waters)

I spent the winter as always now poring over seed catalogues, making plant lists and planting plans. I bought certified organic seed from Seeds of Change and Greta's Organic Gardens and a mix of seed, organic when it was available, from Richter's. I also ordered trays of French lavender, *Echinacea pallida*, St. John's wort, wormwood, feverfew, hyssop, anise hyssop, angelica, skullcap, valerian, arnica and comfrey. I really wanted to find out more about these medicinal herbs and to see how they grew in this soil.

It was a mild winter. Joe blew out the laneway just once, and then only because guests were coming. The previous winter had called for about ten blow-outs. We rather missed the snowshoe treks in the backwoods, and the creek was impassable. We had frequent visits from gaggling flocks of wild turkeys, recently reintroduced to southern Ontario and now proliferating. Otherwise, wildlife sightings were few; the usual deer were scarce, and the lack of snow meant few tracks to observe. Spring was wet, and early attempts to get out there with the tiller were doomed to failure with the mud clogging the tiller and sometimes even freezing. I spread horse manure that Jamie delivered on Gundi's garden and on two extensions of it: a new vegetable area and a new perennial garden area. The latter was being newly reclaimed from years of growth of deep-rooted and clumpy grass. It took several tough tilling sessions to break down, but the spring melt left it waterlogged, especially at the lowest points, for many weeks in April and May. The vegetable area eventually tilled up like butter, while the perennial part remained fairly gooey. In March, the garlics poked their noses up and sniffed the air. Late and frequent frosts cracked the earth and caused the garlic to heave somewhat.

I poked the exposed bulbs back down but was concerned by the wetness. Eventually, in May and June, it all shot up, with a marked difference in vigour between Ted's garlic and the sickly remains of my planting stock from last year, which had yielded small to very small bulbs. It was an interesting comparison, proof (as if I needed it) that healthy seed stock does indeed produce a stronger harvest.

In April and May, I opened up a whole new area at the top east of the field below Gundi's garden, my new market field. In May already, my second season at the Campbellford Farmers Market began, and for the first few weeks, I was very thin on the ground, as the year's crops hadn't even been planted yet! I went on my annual trip to Richter's and loaded up with trays of seedlings. Late May was a frantic time of tilling and preparing rows for planting and seeding.

Heavy hay mulching worked well again this year, at least for all the lavender. The rosemary had finally been choked off in about February, as the length of the winter got to it, so I was left with not one of my eighty or so plants! The lemon balm, oregano, sage, thyme and spearmint were all fine, as was the bergamot, now fully recovered from its fall mildew and raring to go. In this second year, it grew tall and pleased us with a multicoloured display of beautiful flowers. Most pleasing of all was the bumper harvest of English and French lavenders. They seem to truly flourish in the dry, stony soil and the dry conditions.

This was another hot summer, even hotter than the last. There were long dry periods, but, unlike last year, the rains did come eventually, with a memorable six inches of steady rains in one swoop at the end of July. The garlic responded well and was the next harvest after the lavender. Gundi's second daughter Claudia's wedding to Pete was at the beginning of August, so I agonized over when to pull the garlic, settling on doing it on my return mid-month. This proved ideal, and we were able to lay it out to dry in the sun and wind. The hot summer and then late rain gave a good, if unspectacular, harvest. The red Russians and rocamboles eclipsed the seed I had earlier. Next up were the sunflowers. They grew tall and a little spindly but generated a great variety for several weeks in August and September. They sold well but not hugely at the market. I felt the strains of sunflowers I had chosen yielded some flowers that lacked robustness, and I planned to make the choice of better strains a priority in years to come. The fluffy double teddy bear variety proved very popular. Unfortunately, I only got one week of blooms out of it. Fatefully, this was the week my sister Jenny and niece Anna came to visit from the old country, a hot week. Anna helped me to harvest, and Jenny, her leg in a plaster cast protecting a broken ankle, took it to market with me. Through the summer, sales of fresh bunches of herbs were minimal. Where I was successful was with pots of herbs for planting, with lavender as the standout. Dried lavender in little aluminum jars was also popular. Garlic scapes went well for several weeks, ditto Jerusalem artichokes, or sunchokes, in late September and early October.

Overall I was happy with the progress I had made in feeling my way toward a full-time business plan. I certainly loved the work; the clean, fresh air; the fulfillment of breathing in the fragrance and digesting the goodness of fresh produce grown on our own organic land, in our own bountiful soil. I made further progress in May when I embarked on a course in herbal studies which led in a year or so to a diploma through the Australasian College for Herbal Studies (ACHS). I was learning so much so fast about the medicinal and culinary properties of everyday, and not so everyday, herbs. To find the benefits of plants like plantain, yellow dock, dandelion, red clover, alfalfa, goldenrod, burdock, chickweed, fat hen, lamb's quarters, purslane and cleavers that all grow like weeds was eye-opening. Friends and associates were forever curious about the financial viability of my efforts and undertakings. At this early stage, I was under no illusions about the fact that it would take time, and a period of transition, for me to make the farm work as a full-time business from which I could earn a living. In the meantime, I juggled selling and publishing maps and satellite images; helping out with Gundi's glass-sculpture business; sitting as vice-president of the board of our local arts association, Spirit of the Hills; and growing Rolling Hills Organics, all part-time occupations with varying degrees of financial and emotional return. The market-gardening was the most satisfying, but maps remained my bread and butter for the time being. So, as long as I could, I attempted to juggle these balls with a degree of dexterity. When the time was right, I was determined to stride off in my chosen direction. Already a promising new seed, the notion of expanding into growing *Echinacea angustifolia* (purple coneflower) by the acre, had been planted. The price of $30 per pound for the certified organic product through a growing contract was an appealing prospect, and I set to preparing half an acre of the top of the lower field for cultivation the following year. That would mean root harvest in three years. It also seemed time to specialize and find markets for a few crops that could be grown successfully for local sale. In order to sell to the wholesalers and distributors of herbs, I would need to grow in large volume and would be at the mercy of market and price fluctuations, strict quality control, wholesale pricing ... I figured it would be much better to focus on a few high-quality products produced in low volume and branded under our own farm name.

Already I felt vindicated in my efforts to become certified (or verified) organic. The annual inspection led to the inspector's suggestion that we have the entire 25 acres of fields certified organic (the whole workable farm, more or less), all for $300, as opposed to $200 for a couple of acres. That seemed sensible, and the prospect of making a healthy return on the echinacea contract seemed to bear out this wisdom. In March, the farm business was officially registered as "Rolling Hills Organics."

One autumn day, as I was planting garlic, I faced Big Agriculture at our very fenceline. A pungent smell wafted over on the prevailing wind from the field immediately to the west of our main growing area: the smell of liquid manure spread on Joe's adjoining fields. It reeked. I turned the driver back as he brought in his second load and gave him a message for Joe to give me a call. I then called Joe several times; there was no reply. A couple of hours later, Joe came zooming over on his all-terrain Honda but left again without trying to find me in the field. I roared over there. We were both frothing at the mouth.

"I hear you just about had a conniption. Well, you've crossed the line. I have one day a year when I can spread this stuff!" Joe screamed.

"Why today? You can see how windy it is. The smell's blowing right across my fields," I retorted.

"I always win," he raged.

"Look, I'm not stopping you from spreading, just asking you to do it on a less windy day."

"Pete, I'm very busy; I usually do it myself, but this year I contracted it out. They come when they come. That happens to be today, and it happens to be windy."

In the end, we shook hands, both contrite, having seen no sense in jettisoning our neighbourly status. Besides, Gundi and I depended on Joe's snow clearing to get us through the winter. It would be a costly exercise to get it done without him. But boy oh boy did this incident make me realize the interconnectivity of our livelihoods and how big farming practices liked to ride roughshod over the land.

"If you don't like the way we do things, why don't you move back to the city?" Kathy, Joe's wife, tossed out.

Carman had by this time succumbed to liver cancer. His beautiful old farm, just one property beyond Joe's, had been sold to a local acquirer of land for its harvested wood, despite fierce resistance from Carman's son Jamie who had known no home or occupation other than this farm and farming. So disappeared another family farm. The landscape was ripped up in rapid fashion, with the whirring of chainsaws and the sirens of reversing trucks filling the air. In just over a month, the demolition of all designated field fencelines and the grand central avenue had decimated this precious organic resource. And, it was rumoured, sewage sludge could follow on the fields that remained, already looking so bare and vulnerable.

Ah, the family farm. What an evocative concept! Is it all apple pie, fresh-picked veggies on a steaming summer's evening, pickles and preserves? Or is it a hard grind to feed the kids, pay the bills and make ends meet? Like everything, it's usually not black-and-white but somewhere in between; not grey, but all colours of the rainbow.

In days gone by, farms were just handed down from generation to generation as a matter of course, with senior male offspring generally taking over the reins from Pa or Grandpa. This still happened, of course, but more and more often, financial pressures and youthful ambitions caused friction between family members, and working farms were often sold to developers, speculators, industrial farmers and recreational purchasers. Pioneer-built fencelines and hedgerows were regularly uprooted, ploughed under and replaced by mega-fields stretching to the far horizon, created so that men in mega-machinery could flex the muscles of their toys and take their mega-crops to the commodities mega-market. Anybody has a right to buy and sell property, of course, but lost in the process of transferring farmland is the lifeblood and soul of a working farm that traditionally grew many crops and fed a large family, and probably neighbours and friends too. A farmstead in the past would sustain a whole natural lifestyle for a family over generations. The hard graft of all family members and the diverse bounty of the land were aspects of a way of life that was fading into the mists of time. Sad, that. Even sadder is the fact that, given the same love, commitment and devotion that our predecessors invested, these endangered family farms could easily become viable entities once more, feeding modern-day couples, families and friends, local communities and regional customers at markets. The renewed interest in fresh, local foods, with their superior flavour and nutritional value over well-travelled supermarket produce meant that not enough of us were growing foods down on the small local farm. People especially in the large towns and cities around us were developing a hearty appetite for fresh, local food grown holistically *without* the use of toxic fertilizer, pesticides, herbicides and fungicides. They wanted Roundup-free, not Roundup Ready. As a rural community, we needed more people to take on stewardship of the land, work it and tend it with loving care, and tease beautiful, nourishing, pure food from hallowed soil. Some farmers were tired, some had kids with no interest in farming, some had no offspring, and some were looking for apprentices or offering land for lease as were nonfarming landowners. There was a great need for the next generation of farmers to step forward, take a bow and get planting. They would be well appreciated. They would feed grateful customers and help to keep working family farms alive and kicking so that our and future generations could feed off them and thrive. As rural residents, we needed to take on the responsibility of lovingly protecting and managing all the land we could, leaving it in great shape for the next generation of good, honest country farmers and their families to work diligently.

In late autumn, after Thanksgiving, together with new buddy David Acomba (whom I had met at a monthly potluck organized by friends Nina and John), I took on the first of many annual camping and canoeing trips to semi-wilderness parks. Our first was to the dramatic Barron Canyon in Algonquin Park. This formative first-hand experience of Ontario's wealth of natural beauty in her forests, lakes, ancient rock and wildlife inspired me to reflect at the time:

> We bear mute witness to the spirits of the ages,
> masters of this dramatic domain
> dancing wistful on the waters as night descends;
> these custodians of the canyon wrapping us in fog
> as we glide along the waterline, transients,
> water-boatmen on the silky surface,
> a liquid bond straddling the twilit heavens
> and the dark untapped depths beneath our paddles.
>
> Dawn brings light and warmth on a rising breeze,
> the river rippling in playful pirouettes,
> the spirits aglow, etched by shadow,
> surreal countenances, weathered, timeless, craggy,
> guardians of the white and red pines atop the pink, grey boulders,
> the lime-green and yellow lichens, the loons and muskrats,
> hovering, cawing ravens, scurrying mice,
> moose and black bear roaming nearby.

High Up in the Rolling Hills

Over time, spirited seasons guide us onwards,
as the hazy summer days linger ahead of sticky, humid nights;
as, now, the autumnal winds play with leaves all transformation;
as the winter snows will tumble and coat the realm white;
as the bitter storms will rage, then blow out in a whisper;
as the fresh buds of spring will burst forth with fluorescence;
and, forever more, as night snuffs out the light,
till morning rises on the other side of darkness.

5

Echinacea Planting

2003

The lavenders had been protected by heavy hay mulched over the winter, yet there was quite some loss of plants because the woody stems had broken off at the base, we discovered on close inspection in May. It had simply been too cold for too long for them to survive. Even the sage and thyme suffered, particularly the sage I had trimmed back in the fall. On the other hand, the *Echinacea pallida*, St. John's wort, angelica, wormwood, hyssop and comfrey all planted in 2002 sprouted and bushed up well.

I had prepared my first field of *Echinacea angustifolia* by first having the field of wildflowers—previously seeded with a succession of cover crops such as alfalfa, red clover and hairy vetch—ploughed down in the fall. Over the winter, the vegetation had broken down, but with the first thaw and draining in spring, We intensely tilled the entire area with our eight-horsepower BCS rototiller. We staked out rows 100 feet long in an area of 200 feet across, leaving enough space between each row to mow with a 40-inch sickle bar. We then tilled each row several times, ultimately to a good depth, in preparation for 1,500 *Echinacea angustifolia* seedlings, which had been started in a commercial greenhouse in Alberta in February. Gundi, innovative to a fault, created a planting tool which punched out two lines in the soil to receive 20 of the seedlings, each sporting a robust taproot and a first pair of leaves.

At the summer solstice, we threw a party for the planting of our first half acre of echinacea seedlings. People came from near and far to help out. Locals from the Northumberland Hills—a motley array of artists, craftspeople, city professionals, retirees, parents, kids and dogs—were reinforced by old friends from Grimsby, Ancaster, Elora, Newmarket and, of course, Toronto. Those from afar came armed with tents, bug spray, sun lotion and, best of all, some scrumptious dishes for the two-day potluck.

The first planting session began on the Saturday afternoon, just as the first of the summer heat was kicking in. The 50,000 seedlings had arrived in a crate by road the same day as Daniel had arrived from Germany by air. Dan had made first contact with me by e-mail just a few days after I had launched the farm's Web site, www.rollinghillsorganics.com, and a brief exchange of messages tied up the arrangements for him to come and work and stay with us for six weeks, starting just in advance of the planting party. This was bad timing for me to have to pick him up at the airport, as it left Gundi to break into the crate with a crowbar and unload it with little help from the delivery driver. Luckily she did get vital assistance from her glass deliveryman, who happened to arrive at the same time. The shipment had travelled from Alberta over five days of extreme heat and humidity. On top of this, the plant flats had been packed with too little space between the layers, so the plants arrived stressed and turning mushy. Dan and I rigged up a plastic tunnel tent at the suggestion of neighbour and sheep farmer Pat. This enabled us to maintain some plants while we picked others for planting.

So, let the planting begin. Herbalist friend Frank from Elora offered many enthusiastic words of support. A final tilling was followed by the punching out of holes, and the army of ten or so helpers combined to separate the plants and to plant them. Once introduced to their home for the next three summers, each seedling was fed with a sprinkle of nourishing, welcoming water. Victoria and Inga performed the drumming ceremony, and the first 3,000 infants were put to bed for the night, whilst our associates trooped off for an evening of nourishing and invigorating sustenance of our own. Tents were set up, the barbecue was lit, and the balmy night air complemented the sweet scent of freshly cut alfalfa hay in the fields, the fine aura of post-labour languor and views over the rolling hills.

On Sunday morning, the heat drew campers to peer blearily out of tents, and we rustled up a fine breakfast before a crew headed down to the field for the second planting session. Showing the solidarity of great friends, newcomers for the morning Avon and Jamie and their daughters Islay and Faryn had driven from Stratford the night before, stopping at home in Toronto, to be here before heading back beyond Toronto to Oakville in the afternoon. Jamie snapped photos; Avon and the girls planted. Another 3,000 plants were baptized in a few short hours. The heat swelled, and a party of twelve took up the kind offer of Gary and Peter to douse themselves in their swimming pool. The ebullient, refreshed crowd returned for more refreshments before lazily drifting off back to the city, ready for a punishingly hot and sticky workweek. Meantime, the echinaceas made themselves at home and ever so slowly found their feet.

Echinacea pallida

Their pallida cousins, planted the year before in the next field, celebrated the arrival by flaunting their flowers in the wind. They had bushed up remarkably, which augured well for the mass of new kids on the block. We had planted the latter very densely as, being very gregarious, they needed to put all their efforts into producing a solid root mass, this being what we would harvest after three seasons of growth. We could harvest the flowers and seeds in the second year, but the primary marketable commodity is the dried root, which finds its way into certified-organic natural health products, mostly in Europe, especially Germany.

Dan and I built on the grand start provided by the dedicated planters, planting rows 7 to 14 of the 32 with some help from Peter and Gary. This was a dry, hot spell, calling for watering at the end of almost every day. Then came the reinforcement plants. Of the initial 50,000, only 17,000 made it into the ground, the rest moulding before our eyes despite our best efforts to nourish them with air and shade. This next shipment of healthy, vigorous green seedlings, packed in trays with roots bare and no soil arrived in two batches. Each batch arrived overnight in mid-July, giving Dan and me the task of planting 33,000 plants within a few days, keeping the trays cool, preferably refrigerated, and shaded. In eight days in mid-July, we planted the remaining 18 rows, salvaging a matted mush of plants of dubious quality for the last three. And so we ended up with around 45,000 seedlings in the ground. In August, Bill Manske shipped between 5,000 and 10,000 more plants for in-filling. By then Dan had departed, so I had to plant these solo. I found lots of gaps but also lots of spots where shoots were just beginning to poke out of the ground. It was hard to tell if the in-filling was really worthwhile or if it merely doubled up the plants, but, hey, it couldn't do any harm!

Thanks mainly to Dan's sterling help, all the rows of *Echinacea angustifolia* had been planted, although the heat had conspired to get them off to a sluggish start. Now at the end of their first growing season, the plants were preparing for the dormant wintertime. We hoped for vigorous filling out of the leaves, sustained building of the roots, and a harvest of flowers, leaf and seed in the following year.

Weeds came slowly, but they crept along the edges of each row. I undertook a full weeding sweep in August before a 10-day trip to England for our family reunion and celebration of Mum's 80th birthday (and Dad's, although his birthday was earlier in the year). At this time, the garden's productivity was peaking, especially the sunflowers, basil and calendula. There was a poor harvest of lavender this year because of the ravages of last winter, when we had lost about half of the yearlings. We replenished with English and Munstead lavenders. Provençal wasn't available from Richter's this year after their own winter losses. I had also planted plug trays of beautifully robust peppermint, yarrow, valerian, feverfew, anise hyssop, basil and parsley. Cilantro from seed took well, bushed out and provided lots of seed, which I ruined by packaging before it had fully dried. On racks, we air-dried spearmint, peppermint, lemon balm, bergamot, sage, thyme, rosemary, oregano, anise hyssop, comfrey, alfalfa and St. John's wort. A beetle infestation of the St. John's wort had stripped them of their hypericin goodness, leaving the resulting vodka tincture brownish and fairly useless. We made cider-vinegar tinctures with parsley and rosemary. Calendula, chamomile, peppermint and lavender were cold infused into olive or canola oils, and rosemary and comfrey were hot infused. All these herbs were also mixed with beeswax from neighbouring Riverside Farm to make soothing balms and salves.

I sold herbs, cut flowers and herbal products once more at Campbellford Farmers Market and at local specialty stores, and I planned to sell tea mixes, creams and balms through our Web site and also through herbalists and herbal-product manufacturers. For example, Shawla Herbs just up the road was interested in purchasing the fresh harvest of calendula and perhaps valerian and other medicinals. Linda Smith picked a few pounds of the prolific calendula.

Our growing contract with Herbs for your Health stipulated a guaranteed price of $30 per pound of dried root from the *Echinacea angustifolia*. This is not how things worked out. The 50,000 or so seedlings were due to yield dried roots after three growing seasons and a leaf, flower and seed harvest in the second and third years. We furrow-ploughed a second half-acre field in the fall in preparation for planting the following year. Our overall ambitious (or audacious or plain stupid) plan was to open up four half-acre fields that would generate a steady annual income in a couple of years.

On October 1, our 20th wedding anniversary, Gundi and I had the thrill of a floatplane trip up and over our treasured land. It was breathtaking to see our hilltop, rooftop, and then the neat rows of plants, winding creek, marsh and ancient white pine stand all from a height of 500 feet. The 45-minute tour reinforced our attachment to this lovely part of the world. Rice Lake, our launchpad, was a wonder in itself. We immediately pledged to go up again, and to take better pictures of the house and land!

In a world where the news was loaded with stories of acts of random violence and unimaginable cruelty, organized state brutality, religious wars, bloody conflicts and even genocides, we had thrown in the towel one day and moved out to the country. Craving fresh air, peace and quiet, a simpler life, a slower pace and more space, we headed up into these mysterious hills. We feathered our new nest, a hillside homestead and a sizeable (55 acres) chunk of land, and wondered what tomorrow might bring. In uprooting to the country, we had anticipated cultural deprivation and a struggle to make ends meet and to maintain our businesses, passions and pastimes. The rural community we came to was first cautious, then accommodating, then outright welcoming to us.

We began by growing our own food when family farms and growers of natural organic produce were somehow tucked away out of sight. Food was central. We were tired of packaged goods, shopping in oversized supermarkets and being bombarded by advertising and luxury-lifestyle channels on television. I wanted to get my hands dirty, smell the turned-over earth, plant seeds, see their produce trumpet through the weeds and live the organic dream. Strolling through fields of wildflowers; harvesting fresh garlic, juicy tomatoes and herbs; tasting succulent baby greens in the humid heat after a summer thunderstorm—we now did all this. And boy, did it ever taste good! We harvested the sunchokes and rhubarb from the kitchen garden; the Concord grapes from the vine; the wild asparagus, fiddleheads and berries from the back forty; and even heritage apples from the ancient orchard, pressing them into a tangy cider. We collected and dried mints, chamomile, linden blossoms, lavender, alfalfa, goldenrod and juniper berries and made teas from them. We stored potatoes, squash and carrots and made preserves of the summer bounty. In our own backyard we discovered a private garden where we could breathe freely, explore, be endlessly inspired. We fell into rhythm with the changing seasons, poring over catalogues and skating and snowshoeing in the crisp bright days of winter, preparing the ground and planting in the spring, growing and nurturing our babies through the heat of the summer, then sitting back to marvel at the splash of ever-changing colour on the trees as fall caused us to think ahead to winter once more.

We took trips to farmers markets and back-road farms, their offbeat farmers offering grass-fed beef, pastured pork and lamb, free-range chickens, ducks and eggs. We rambled around the countryside, stopping to snap more photos of the fields of round hay bales in the late-afternoon sun and taking in panoramic vistas over farms, small towns and meandering waterways. We explored the back roads with Beethoven's transcendent *Pastoral Symphony* as glorious company. Along the way we experienced epiphanies and magical revelations. Colourful characters and like-minded souls abounded, appearing out of the blue at wacky events like the annual melon tasting in September, the Christmas Eve Orphans from the Storm party, the bocce and broomball tournaments, and the midsummer Long Lunch for 1,500 souls seated side by side along the main street of our vibrant village of Warkworth. And we resolved to stick around for many a year here in these elevating hills.

2004

In June, my good friend Dave Walkinshaw came for a couple of weeks to construct a new cedar deck that would wrap around the back of our house and face out over the fields and hills beyond. With my help, he did a stellar job, and the deck, now naturally weathered by the elements, continues many years later to provide us with a comfortable and expansive space from which to view our lovely peaceful surroundings. The Concord grapevines that previous owner Paul Von Baich had planted were trained into a pergola over the deck, and they now provide necessary shade from the hot summer sun. We enjoy most summer meals here as the birds twitter all around us.

Later in the summer, it rained and rained and rained. It was cool too. The previous year's first planting of echinacea didn't do much after its partial pretty bloom at the end of June. Toby helped me weed, then was an indispensable help in planting my second half acre in the cool between August's rains. It was an average year for harvests and sales. The Campbellford Farmers Market limped along, with sales of the original trinity of garlic, lavender and sunflowers leading the way. I ventured to open a Warkworth Summer Market on the urging of Paulus who was opening Frantic Farms glass and pottery gallery in the village, to be joined by a bakery alongside, in the old Laundromat building he had purchased. Sales initially flourished thanks to a mail-drop flyer which made the locals check us out but then tapered off. Tuesdays and Thursdays there and Saturdays in Campbellford meant a total of three days a week of markets. But for Toby's willingness to man the stand for most of the duration, it would have been too much. Frequent showers and thunderstorms didn't help. Teas and salves and Northumberland satellite images supplemented the herb plants and sundry greens, as did a few items from other growers like strawberries, bedding plants and potatoes. My green trailer, which Dan had constructed and painted last year, was a popular display at both markets.

6

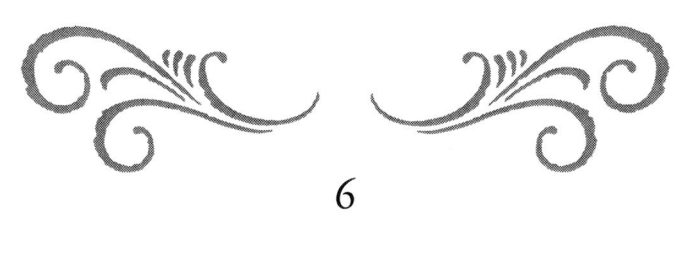

Co-operative Years

2005

I had decided during the winter, over the course of several lengthy meetings, to join the newly formed Quinte Organic Farmers Co-operative. This was an opportunity to really grow and market that I felt I could not afford to pass up. I could continue to put the name Rolling Hills Organics out there and build production and sales through farmers markets and wholesale accounts, but I felt I was ultimately better off looking to consolidate to local markets, including the lucrative Toronto one, that were only really open to our young farm if we were part of a larger entity.

At the beginning of May, after furrow-ploughing the area, we planted around 4,000 tree seedlings on five acres up the hill. They were a mix of white pine, red pine, European larch and Norway spruce. The poor saplings then had to endure weeks without rain and considerable early summer heat. I could only manage the trees by sickle-bar cutting between the rows; not a simple task by midsummer when they had grown in.

Hot on the heels of the tree planting came the season of growing and marketing produce through the co-op, and I decided to offer lettuce, several salad mixes, arugula, beets, basils, cilantro, calendula and sunflowers, all grown from seed. The garlic planted last November was the first to break the wet surface in March. Lenni at Art Farm in Warkworth started curly and Italian parsleys, sage, thyme and oregano from seed for me in her greenhouse. And I purchased English lavender and rosemary plug trays from Richter's. My first foray to Riverdale Farmers Market in Toronto came on the first Tuesday of May. Gundi helped me out the first day, and we were so tickled at our sales tally that we went out to celebrate with friends Chris and Allan. The season started with asparagus and rhubarb. It hit a bump when the strawberry season was cut short at around ten days by the prolonged dry spell and intense heat. It turned into a hot, dry summer that was bad for peas, berries, lettuce, brassicas and more. However, I was more than happy with the increased sales of arugula and salad-greens mixes through the co-op. I succession-planted through the summer, and it kept going to October. Fresh herbs (parsleys, basils, rosemary, sage, thyme and oregano) sold so-so, but lavender plants and flowers sold well. The garlic and sunflower harvests were disappointing. Other co-op growers offered fresh lamb, cherry and field tomatoes, strawberries while they lasted, asparagus, sweet corn and sweet potatoes.

On top of what we sold at the Riverdale market, Rolling Hills Organics sent out fresh herbs, arugula and salad greens in volume to Village Market in Toronto and, to a lesser extent, to Campbellford and Belleville farmers markets. This made for busy days of picking, washing, spinning, weighing, bagging and delivering every Friday in peak season, but it was wonderful to have my weekends free and my regular summer Friday evening game of soccer in Peterborough in the Over 35s (Old Timers!) league. I really enjoyed the mix of growing and selling, particularly the positive feedback from Toronto's organic food consumers who loved having the opportunity to buy food picked fresh that morning and delivered direct from the farm. Farmers market sales for our own small farm more than doubled this year because of the co-op's four markets. The following year, these markets could double sales again, I hoped. Continuous doubling of sales each year is clearly unsustainable growth, but the good news at this juncture was that the burgeoning organic food market was in demand and undersupplied. If we grew it, hopefully under more favourable conditions than we experienced this year, we should certainly be able to sell it.

With August came echinacea-planting time, but only of 25,000 plants on a quarter acre. I had prepared a new half-acre plot by furrow-ploughing last fall and cultivating several times in the spring and dry early summer to break down all the grass and weed growth. Then I planted buckwheat and ploughed it under as it flowered. I cultivated the lower half of the new plot to break down the buckwheat and planted fall rye on it in September. On the upper half of the plot, I planted echinacea after cultivation. With concern I had noted leafhoppers on the first field last year. I was very disturbed to see them return and spread to the second field this year. An introduction of ladybugs didn't seem to help much, and neither did separate sprayings of neem and garlic water. The first few rows of the second field had been a glorious sight in late June and early July: the plants robust, the flowers a pretty sight indeed.

Our half acre of Echinacea angustifolia in full bloom

But later in the summer, the leaves began to discolour and die back. I decided not to harvest the first field as I had planned when planting it two summers back. Another season of weeding was a daunting prospect, but I hoped the plants would recover and the roots fill out.

DAD'S PASSING

Dad stayed in constant touch and kept right up to date on my latest. A year after a walk on Kinver Ridge to view his proposed resting place, it was time to visit Mum and Dad. Acutely aware of his vulnerability after several minor heart attacks, Dad had for a while been tying up loose ends, putting his affairs in order and making arrangements. I spent a week with them at their home in Bournville, in south Birmingham. This week, to be his last, was filled with bright, sunny days and cold, frosty nights. Dad was full of his usual mix of thoughtful musings and happy banter. He paid homage to the fallen ones throughout the week leading up to Remembrance Day. He made his usual care-giving calls to ailing friends and neighbours. He reviewed and updated the Finch and Mullins family histories, talking glowingly about his mother and father. He was thrilled to make the first sale of his poetry collection. He listened to the cricket on the radio. He revelled in Chopin nocturnes and Mozart piano concertos. He even burst into song more than once as he showed me his revised funeral service program.

The family enjoyed meals together. We picked and ate the last raspberries from the garden. We went for sunny walks in the park. My sisters and I reminisced about our childhoods, happy times for him and for us. Above all he was overjoyed to spend time with his closest family—his beloved Mary, his daughter Jill visiting from Berlin and me from Canada, daughter Jenny and her husband Bob, granddaughters Anna and Sarah, all of whom had been constantly close by for Jack and Mary in recent years. All of us were with him on what turned out to be his last evening. Just grandchildren Mieke and Janko and my wife, Gundi, were sadly not with us at this time.

Then, on a sunny afternoon stroll in the park with Jill, a massive heart attack struck him down and Dad suddenly took leave of us, a contented soul with an enlarged heart filled with love. His spirit will live on in all those that he touched with his humility and boundless love for people everywhere. His journey continued as he moved on to Kinver Edge, where the earth meets the heavens for him. From there, it was on to the great beyond. He had told me that death held no fear for him. He believed that it would reunite him with loved ones that had gone before.

A plaque on a bench up on Kinver Edge in memory of another departed one reads:

May the winds of love blow softly
On this quiet and peaceful place
Where our loved one
Will never be forgotten.

As another year wound down and I looked outside at the snow-blanketed fields below the house, it was hard for me to envisage the rush of spring growth in a few months. I was somewhat overwhelmed by growing, picking, markets, maps and bookkeeping this last summer, and it took time to regroup. With my November visit to England and Dad's sudden passing at the end of my week there, I was left in a bit of a fog, one which lingered awhile. I didn't find time to handle all those end-of-season chores like hay-mulching the lavender and garlic, bringing in the garden hoses and tools, doing maintenance on the rototiller, parking and covering up the tractor ... The cold came early and sharp. Winter blew in like a slap in the face.

2006

It would have been fanciful to hope to wind up my 20 or so years of map publishing and distribution through my map business on an even keel. As I turned 50 (entering my third quarter!), I looked forward to a good few years of physical outdoor growing pursuits, and maybe earning a content little living along the way. The plan at this time was to focus on *fresh-local-organic* as the byword, and marketing specialty products to a niche audience seemed a fine way to go. Herbalists, natural-health buffs, organic-food lovers and appreciative chefs, stores and resorts, all of whom shared the passion for sustainability and practicality, would hopefully provide the main markets for what I loved to grow—medicinal and culinary herbs, gourmet greens, colourful happy flowers. There was a wave of enthusiasm for fresh foods sourced close to home, and I was excited by the prospects for the future with such buoyancy in the air.

An alternative to food from industrial-sized mega-farms that travelled vast distances by truck was possible. Back in 2002 Frederick Kirschenmann, Director of the Leopold Center for Sustainable Agriculture in Iowa, had written that "The rapid development of farmers' markets, direct markets, and markets for organically produced foods all point to changes in the marketplace that have the potential to develop a new direction for food and farming. A growing segment of the consuming public has signaled that they want to know where their food comes from, how it was produced, how the animals were treated, and whether or not the food was produced using good environmental stewardship."

As food-borne illnesses and diet-related diseases and their relationship to our industrial food processes become part of the public consciousness, food shoppers increasingly look for opportunities to form relationships with farmers with whom they can have conversations about the food they eat. This is part of a larger trend toward the "experience economy" in which co-operative relationships are key. New technologies make it possible for independent, moderate-sized farmers to link with local processors to establish such relationships and thereby gain a competitive advantage over consolidated firms. This system has the potential to make a major contribution to producing healthy, well-balanced diets in some of the world's regions of rapidly growing populations as well as in North America.

Food customers have a say in what their local landscapes look like through the food choices they make. The relationships they create in their quest for more healthy food will also lead to increased awareness of the other public services these farmers provide: properly managed soils help filter water and improve water quality; properly managed landscapes provide habitats for wildlife, helping to restore biodiversity and to provide recreational space for well-regulated hunting and fishing. This awareness will make it easier to rally citizens behind the policy changes needed to support these farmers.

Over recent years, our collective aspirations of creating a more just world based on fair trade and respect have been obstructed by the merchants of war and greed. Financial downturns and crises have confirmed the realization that our problems are global in scope and that we are all affected. Fear, depression, hunger and despair take hold as prices escalate, debt increases and unjust laws and practices continue around the world. Globally, whole cultures face the choice of using the ongoing financial and food crises to grow into more mature, consensus-driven, sharing societies or retrenching into top-down protectionism, fierce competition and cruel exclusion, all at the expense of the environment.

Around the world, towns and villages are already attempting to reclaim their communities and to trade locally on a manageable scale. Fair trade, micro-financing, the empowerment of women, renewable energy and jobs, conservation and recycling all contribute to enable the shift. Transition times call for community-building. Transition Towns initiatives kick off when a small collection of motivated individuals within a community come together with a shared concern of responding to the challenges and opportunities of fossil-fuel dependency and climate change. A significant proportion of the people in a community is needed to plan a Transition Town. They need to mobilize and work together to increase resilience and drastically reduce carbon emissions and general waste so that the community can sustain itself and thrive. Even if there were any doubt about the extent of fossil-fuel depletion and the causes of climate change projected by scientists, in order to avoid potential disaster, it is sheer folly not to act according to the precautionary principle. Near our home, Peterborough has recently taken a lead in Canada. The initiative's operative guideline is to achieve the balanced reduction in energy consumption and switch to renewable energy sources by reducing emissions by 5 percent annually until 2020. The proposed infrastructure is a new essential and balanced economy. Its focus is resilience through energy reduction leading to sustainability.

We are fortunate in a community such as ours to have a head start in community building and nurturing. Arts groups, grassroots organizations, service groups, community foundations, progressive publications, centres of learning and co-operatives all provide forums for engagement. Our communities are endowed with artisans and artists (ecological builders, bakers, candle makers, woodworkers, architects, farmers, gardeners, designers, writers, actors, musicians, dancers, painters, sculptors, potters, weavers, photographers, filmmakers and therapists among them). There are merchants, promoters and catalysts right in our midst. Still needed are yet more community builders and shapers, a lot more cohesive, forward-thinking planning from our municipalities, and more bodies to populate our local communities over time, to allow it to evolve and flourish. We need to grow and consume more locally, using the land to produce organic food from the heart, the way communities used to. We need to train young people and retain their energy and ideas. And we need to conserve nature and wildlife, develop land gradually and sensibly, transitioning from manufacturing to a diversified economy focusing on renewable energy, enlightened farming, trading, educating, health care, tourism and other service industries.

Bold far-sighted policy planning and practice at all levels now would lead to a successful, vibrant economy and environment. Given global communication networks, there is endless opportunity for individual engagement, with transformation of communities over time the goal.

7

A Health Scare

In March and April we spent a few days on the Pacific in Zihuatanejo, then three weeks in Patzcuaro, Mexico, soaking up the atmosphere of a lively old Michoacan town. On return from Mexico City, Gundi was ill—very, very ill—for several months.

She came home with "a bug," experiencing bloody diarrhoea since the last days of Patzcuaro. Bacteria? Parasites? A virus? They were the same symptoms she had had several times before: after our first trip to Chile together, after Oaxaca and once or twice in between. Homeopathic and naturopathic treatments had always seen it away in the past, but this time it really took hold. Nothing helped, and the debilitating, energy-sapping loss of blood continued for several weeks. At the end of April, it was time to go to the emergency room in Campbellford. The duty doctor prescribed antibiotics to deal with what was assumed to be Mexican parasites or bacteria. Over the next week, Gundi's symptoms worsened, so it was time for her to go to the emergency room again. The back wheel had come off the car on my drive into Warkworth on Saturday, so before dawn on that Sunday morning in early May, I had to call an ambulance after Gundi had another night of heavy blood loss. She was given blood tests and an ECG, then admitted to hospital for two days.

Three weeks passed with Gundi back home. May 30 was a hot and tiring day for me at Riverdale farmers market. A bladder infection began for her that night. The next morning she saw our family doctor, Jacob, and he prescribed antibiotics for the infection. A few days later Gundi was still very weak, so I drove her in to the emergency room. She received blood transfusions and was admitted to hospital again, where she was put on intravenous medication. The overzealous and gruff visiting surgeon from Peterborough wanted to whip out part of her colon. After five days, she was discharged, and we went straight to Peterborough for her first visit with gastroenterologist Dr. Chow. There had been some wait time for an appointment with him but an even longer wait to see two other gastroenterologists in the regional centre of Peterborough. Dr. Chow inhabited a windowless office and perfunctorily entered data into his computer. He avoided eye contact and dodged any personal observations about his patient's health. He practiced medicine as a pure, definitive science and deflected personal (irrational?) concerns. "You are ill and probably will be for some considerable time to come. Take these medications; you will need to stay on them for a very long time," was his blunt message. He re-prescribed the heavy medication Gundi had been given on her last visit to hospital. We went home, tired but willing. Since her discharge from Campbellford Hospital, home-care nurses (from the Victorian Order of Nurses) were coming in seven days a week.

After five more tired days at home, we finally got Gundi to her first visit with Dr. James Yuan, practitioner of traditional Chinese medicine and herbalist in Toronto. Daughter Cristina and I were with Gundi on her first visit, when she could barely make it into the city on a steaming hot day. Dr. Yuan was a soft-spoken, gentle man who oozed compassion. He tested her pulse, examined her tongue, felt her stomach, pinched her skin, and looked deeply into his patient's eyes, all to ascertain her energy levels. He asked Gundi how she felt, how her energy levels were, what her symptoms were. He then prescribed a mix of 12 Chinese herbs and other medicinals—roots, seeds, leaves, flowers, bark, shell, bone, cartilage—and gave directions for their preparation (two very strong cups of tea to be drunk every day for six days). The apothecary then mixed the herbs, dividing them into one paper bag for each day. A week later, Gundi returned and reported on her condition. He then prescribed a new mix of herbs based on the underlying condition and changes. This was to continue until the patient no longer needed any herbs to get better or to stay healthy. Dr. Yuan and his team of assistants, mostly Asian women, were immensely caring, personable and demonstrative.

Gundi noticed an improvement already the next day. Then, after four days, the bleeding amazingly stopped, finally, after all this time—six long weeks. No miracle, it was eminently explainable: the treatment worked. Then she had a relapse, and after several weeks in Peterborough Hospital, Gundi was given her first thorough colonoscopy in late June (which she was excited to watch on a full-colour monitor). It revealed several polyps, which were all removed. Gastroenterologist Dr. Chow conducted the colonoscopy himself. Inflammation was down. On the July Canada Day long weekend, Gundi recovered more mobility and was taken off IV medication. Dr. Chow officially discharged her, but she opted to stay in hospital for another two days to recover more strength. She returned home on July 3. Hallelujah! Home-care services provided by the public health system continued. Authorities then cut back the home visits to four days, then one day a week before terminating them. We were grateful to be granted a drug plan which allowed for free prescriptions as long as home care lasted.

This time in our lives was immensely challenging. I can only begin to imagine how Gundi coped with those endless days and lonely nights in two hospitals and with the depletion of her reserves of energy. I was single-minded in my determination to see her through this episode and help her to recharge her system after the storm passed through. "Rugged Resilient Winners," I had jotted down on a Post-it stuck to my computer monitor to spur us on. In truth, I couldn't face the desperate alternative. I felt I had to take charge of events in a rational yet supremely caring way, for my love, my essence as a human being, was under threat. It was invigorating and gratifying to come though such a battle. It made us feel stronger, more loving and more together than ever. Communicating Gundi's condition to others was not easy since friends and family were so concerned. Each person had a different view of it and varied advice. But aren't we fortunate that they cared so! To have faced this ordeal alone would have been punishing. The human frailty that health problems reveal makes us ultimately more humane, more alive, bringing us closer. We are so fragile yet so strong; we bend, but it is hard to break us. And our spirit of caring carries us through crises, passings, mournings and recuperations out into the warm embrace of healing and belonging. In adversity, life shines through, an infinite beacon. We had Gundi's eldest daughter Cristina and many wonderful friends to thank, and my sister Jill and friend David talked with me and guided me through the dark times.

Visitors came and went in a blur to me, including Cristina (for six weeks); Claudia and Sofie; Neil from England (for my cancelled 50th birthday celebrations); Vicky and Gary from California; Ulli from Germany (for two weeks); Andrea, Lake and Brady; Aaron, Melanie and Pete; and Victoria. Gundi's team of caregivers included Linda Greenwood, Linda Zeisner, Nina, Arlene and Mike, Gary and Peter, Heidi, Skye, Sandy, Kevin, Chris and

Allan, Greg and Sally and the VON nurses who came in to help in between hospital stays in Campbellford and Peterborough.

All the while we strove to be very careful with diet, but after hospital food and the tediously bland meals the regular "nutritionist" recommended, Gundi was champing at the bit for more satisfying fare. The main thing, according to Dr. Yuan, was to avoid spicy and cold foods, and alcohol. It was so gratifying to see Gundi's appetite gradually return, yet it seemed to take an age before she could regain any weight. We celebrated when the scale showed a one-pound increase! Her weight had gone down at one alarming point to a mere 106 pounds, an immensely distressing sight. In happier days, we got back to celebrating a one-pound decrease.

We made visits to naturopath Dr. Hania Armengol in Ottawa in November and December. We had been disappointed when Gundi's condition flared up so violently back in April that the homeopathic and naturopathic treatments Hania had prescribed did not bring the symptoms under control as they had done previously. There was some miscommunication with Hania at the time, which resulted in critical delays in receiving prescriptions, so who knows what might have been. Gundi wanted to go back to Hania when she felt better and had come off all medications prescribed by Dr. Chow. (Dr. Chow had recommended in October that she stay on the same heavy daily dose of anti-inflammatory drugs for a long time to come, maybe forever!) The medical establishment represented by Dr. Chow had lumped Gundi's condition into the general classification of irritable bowel syndrome. Hania chatted with Gundi about her condition and feelings, then examined her. She noted that her system was fairly depleted and prescribed five liquid micromineral preparations to be taken as drops for one month. She felt that parasites Gundi had picked up in Mexico were the trigger for her depleted system and subsequent illness. After a few days of taking the preparations, Gundi felt much better. A follow-up appointment confirmed considerable improvement, so Hania gave a new prescription. Gundi continued to improve. By December she had turned the corner and her weight was back to 135 pounds. Thank goodness.

For many weeks, Cristina had done valiant work in Gundi's garden and planted vegetables. I kept on keeping on with weeding, planting, picking, washing, spinning, packaging, ordering, preparing, then going into Toronto weekly to sell at the Riverdale market. I had sparse help, from Dave from Vancouver for just a few weeks and from Caroline before she too left. Local boys Kevin and Patrick helped for several days picking rocks and ripping up the worst of the weeds, allowing the echinacea plants to breathe somewhat. Fields of them, especially the lower field, had looked glorious in late June and early July, but I was to find the work of harvesting the roots through a sodden fall extremely disheartening, as the low volume barely warranted the work it took. A happier story was the bountiful harvest of arugula, salad mixes, parsleys, lavender, garlic, radishes and sunflowers. Total sales at Riverdale were up around 40 percent over last year, so the hard summer paid off in material terms. I had put all I had into it, and every night I collapsed into bed, mentally and physically exhausted.

Kawartha Highlands

Charged up, we set off at sunrise for our annual camping and canoeing trip, the landscape dusted in white. It was early November. The wind howled, but the day started bright, with ice covering the front grille of the car as we strapped on the canoe in Lakefield.

Our load was heavy—tent, sleeping bags, food and drink for four days, clothing, backpacks, firewood. Off we paddled into a stiff wind ploughing down Long Lake. Three mean portages and five hours later, we arrived at our recommended campsite for the duration, a lovely location facing up and down two arms of Stoplog Lake on a rocky promontory.

The view from our campsite

A change of scenery, a change of pace getting out there in nature, away from people, distraction, the routine of daily life. Just two pals in a groove, tuning in to a wild location as the view all around us—the foliage, the lake, the weather—transformed by the minute. A mad mix of rain, wind, squalls, sleet, snow, hail, roving clouds, clear breaks of blue sky and sunshine, night-time constellations reflected in the still water, misty mornings, frost, drizzle. We sat wrapped up and toasty by the glowing campfire, nourished by hearty food and red wine, morning coffee and eggs. We conversed, mused, reminisced wistfully about Gundi's illness, our departed fathers and David's recently departed mother, chuckled, joked, smoked cigars, read poetry, planned, laughed our socks off.

We were challenged, but we were up to it. We gave thanks and revelled in the moment, especially seated on the thunder box in the morning and perched on our cliff at sundown. These days cleared out our pent-up minds and sent tingles coursing through our veins. We were pumped.

The rhythm of the paddles plying through the waters was satisfying, like a steady, sound heart beating away. As we plunged the paddle, the earth slowly moved, the shore changed, and the water parted for us. The rain pounded drops onto the surface in a constant bombardment on every square foot in our sights. It trickled through layers of clothing all the way down to booted feet; finally, damp became wet became drenched compounded by cold. Over treacherous interminable steep portages, we lugged our belongings and the canoe that has cradled us on the water one more time back to Long Lake and the final, long trial of a leg back to base. Soaked, chilled and tired, we landed in our real world and changed into our cozy selves again. In a toasty pub in Port Burleigh, I chuckled as I watched my beloved football team, United, win in Europe.

Also in November I got around to completing my first harvest of *Echinacea angustifolia* roots. It was wet, cold, and tedious work washing them. They were placed on newly-built racks in the shed and fan-heated for a few days to speed up drying. My contracted buyer, Bill Manske, made himself scarce, saying that the big buyers would not be purchasing until spring at the earliest. He warned me that large manufacturers wanted large volume and had driven the price down from $30 per pound to a miserly $5. The mega-manufacturers had apparently ruined the promising market for certified organic root. I had visited Faunus Herbs' facility two years before, and an order from them for spring materialized. As soon as the ground was workable, I dug some fresh root, but proposed delivery of dried root by mid-May was late for the buyer, so they took some fresh, some partially dried. I was disappointed that they still had some later in the year and so didn't need any new fresh root in the fall. All in all, my "guaranteed" lucrative echinacea business had turned into a bit of a bust. With an early freeze, I was unable to fill an order of fresh root in late November. The customer settled on dried root left over from last year's harvest, which was nice, and the customer complimented the quality. After my visit to Faunus, I had backed off on weeding of the echinacea fields and merely sickle-barred between the rows. I ploughed the top field under in the spring and planted buckwheat there in August. This was ploughed under in early October to ready the field for full greens production.

Over recent years I had shifted my role from full participation in international commerce, travel and interaction to one more cautiously concentrated on my locality. I had enjoyed peddling maps and satellite images, which, to my mind, acted as base sources of objective information upon which each purchaser could build or extend his or her world view. Some images were new and exciting, like the *GeoSphere Image, Living Earth* and *Earth at Night* whole Earth satellite views. My Mum had the prescience to send me an article from *The Guardian* newspaper describing the GeoSphere Project, California sculptor Tom Van Sant's vision of producing the first ever composite satellite view of the entire planet. I read and reread the article and found Tom's phone number through directory inquiries. After an invigorating conversation, I found myself, at Tom's suggestion, on a flight bound for Los Angeles to meet with him at his beachside studio in Santa Monica. Before I knew it, I had secured publishing rights to the images for Canada and Europe for our map company. Within months came a proud highlight of my professional life—the sale of 23,000 world satellite-image posters published by my own company in response to an offer published in the *London Sunday Times Magazine* on the very day that the first Gulf War broke out. For several years we trotted off to the Frankfurt Book Fair every October as exhibitors, showcasing regular and enlarged posters of *The Earth from Space* to prospective distributors.

The image certainly struck a chord with those who viewed this groundbreaking view of the world. I was privileged to have subsequently been involved with the publication and dissemination of tens of thousands more whole Earth satellite images over several years when they were truly novel. Some images merely depicted the world as it had been charted by Western cartographers, like *National Geographic* maps. It was sad to see interest in the pure objective satellite images being eclipsed by the subjectivity of political maps. The novelty of seeing our physical world from space, without any annotation to guide us, slowly wore off, and interest in following exploding geopolitical conflicts and wars turned people back to maps chock full of information and detail as they asked questions such as, Where in the world is Afghanistan? The information displayed on maps was seen from a Western perspective and increasingly sanctioned by Western governments, as were the entire agendas of nations and their conflicts. In the name of security, we were being force-fed censored information and blatant propaganda. Some 20 years later, world views have been further transformed by open access on our computers and cell phones to extremely high resolution images of Earth down to street level. These images have acted as a powerful magnifying glass applied to our physical world at every level. The staggering detail of yet higher resolution classified images now offers military strategists and espionage operations unfettered access to the movements of people everywhere on the planet, with unmanned drones now acting with impunity to take out so-called security threats without due process. In this sense, satellite imagery has become an overtly political tool, far from the pure means for exploring the wonders of the world that had attracted me.

So I had retreated to the hills here to work my plot, venturing out occasionally to inhale the vibrancy and life of other locales. For example, we returned from the Mexican pueblo, just as the Iraqi village was being pounded into submission for a second time, in preparation for years of occupation as a base for other exploits in the region. The invaders' new regime sanctioned the pre-emptive strike and unilateral action, and the peaceful coexistence of nations of the world was being thwarted by a vengeful beast of a superpower. It seemed to be down to special interest groups, nongovernmental organizations, grassroots movements and alternative media around the world to make their voices heard, reaffirm their views, and continue to stand firm in their common belief that dialogue and diplomacy are the key tools in dealing with international issues. The nations of the world seemed preoccupied at this point in history with organizing themselves into highly militarized geopolitical blocs and spheres of influence, even a New World Order, with an obsessive lust for power and control. Back in 1961, President Dwight Eisenhower had warned against such developments in his farewell speech to the people of the United States: "In the councils of government, we must guard against the acquisition of unwarranted influence, whether sought or unsought, by the military-industrial complex. The potential for the disastrous rise of misplaced power exists and will persist."

Peter Finch

During this year I completed 50 years on earth. I should have learned something worthwhile by now! My attempt to record experiences and learnings, leanings and yearnings gathered steam. As I looked back over paths travelled, fresh prospects came into focus.

8

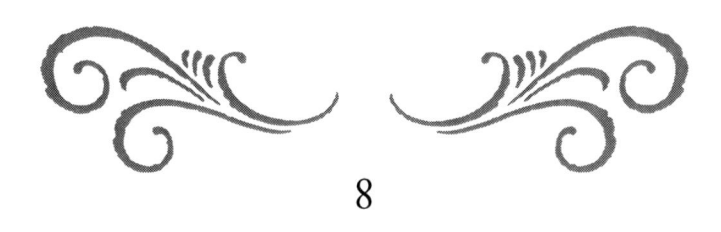

Trust Nature

"Trust Nature." The words jumped off the page and danced around my head for a few minutes. It was like fireworks going off, on and on, like those Nietzsche aphorisms which were just so simple, so pure and so enduring.

Trusting nature is what we just can't seem to do collectively. Politicians; economists; mining, chemical and pharmaceutical companies; the corporate world and religious leaders all vehemently deny her and build whole belief systems and faiths to keep her excluded from their world of power, pomp and circumstance. Why? Fear, I suppose, is at the root of it, fear of doing themselves out of a job, fear of ultimate truths. They have all propagated the myth of a world based on the conquest and suppression of nature in order to establish the control and power they crave. But the myth is a transparent veil. It has been going on ever since the early Europeans brought arrogance and greed to the New World, plundering the land and killing off the natives. By the 19th century, commercial hunting succeeded in wiping out the vast herds of buffalo (American bison) that roamed the Great Plains, starving natives of a principal food source, forcing them to move away from their ancestral lands and onto reservations.

It kept coming back to me: *Trust Nature!* Previously it had been human life that was sacred (in the words of Dr. Dixon, the Unitarian minister who married Gundi and me). But it goes beyond that. It is nature that is sacred and deserves our trust in its raw form. We must get beyond the view of humanity as apart from the natural realm, as it is only by working in harmony with nature that we can make progress toward a future that is sustainable. Are we moving from the Holocene into the Anthropocene Era? Some geologists now believe that human activity has so irrevocably altered our planet that we have entered a new geological age. Over the last 11,700 years—an epoch that geologists call the Holocene—climate has remained remarkably stable. This allowed humans to plan ahead, inventing agriculture, cities, communication networks and new forms of energy.

But industrial powers of destruction have led us into times of great upheaval and shift, making them the new normal. Once we exhaust species of plants and animals in their natural habitats, they are gone forever, even though they have been around, evolving in subtle ways, for millions of years. What a sad record our generation will leave our descendants, a record of greed, woeful short-term planning, lack of foresight and outright blindness to a bigger picture and action beyond instant gratification. Exclusion of nature from all but sanctimonious, short-lived acknowledgements of a few pieces of undeniable beauty—a magnificent mountain range, a thundering waterfall, a brilliant sunset, an erupting volcano—can lead only to devastating, irreversible loss.

There are, of course, those of us heathens who swim against the tide and not only trust but truly revere nature. We are in awe in her presence and love her brute force, her adaptability, unpredictability, endurance, complexity and sheer sensuousness. We never lose our child's sense of amazement, and we feel an irresistible inner connection to her workings. We want to immerse ourselves in her swirling rapids, dance in her sultry breezes and lose ourselves in her fragrant forests. We have a touching link with the primeval; we belong there with her. We have all lived that supreme moment when the wild envelops us in a warm blanket and moves us to our very soul. We feel that incredible sense of belonging. Yet, most feel impelled to go back to the constructed human world distanced and divorced from nature. We incorporate little mementoes of her into our daily lives as reminders that we really do care, but it is sad how small and how shallow is most people's everyday connection with nature. Children now grow up with nature deficit disorder: Most fresh foods on offer at the supermarket are tainted by chemical additives and toxins; the processed foods we eat are loaded with synthetic substances; the air we are forced to breathe and the municipal tap water we are supplied to drink are both polluted by industry's toxic chemicals; the cures we are prescribed for our sicknesses are generally chemical, poisonous, addictive. Unless we are vigilant, the products we buy to ostensibly maintain our bodies, homes and environments are largely unnatural and actually harmful to our health. Again, there are those of us who wake up to the clarion call of the wild and opt to restrict our purchases to natural, organically produced materials and hope that others will follow suit.

Nature deserves to have rights enshrined in law, as indigenous peoples around the world know well. Article 1 of the new "Rights for Nature" chapter of the Ecuadorian constitution reads: "Nature, or *Pachamama*, where life is reproduced and exists, has the right to exist, persist, maintain and regenerate its vital cycles, structure, functions and its processes in evolution. Every person, people, community or nationality will be able to demand the recognitions of rights for Nature before the public bodies."

Like Ecuador's, forward-looking governments in Costa Rica, Cuba and Bhutan have been putting their houses in order by working hard to conserve nature. Nations with big, vital geographies like Canada, Brazil, Russia, China, Greenland, Indonesia and, yes, the United States of America would do well to step up their own sustainable visions for the future.

2007

We were not through this yet.

Gundi never looked completely recovered, yet we were so thrilled that her energy had gotten back to normal. She was exercising, back to doing yoga weekly, working away on her glass sculptures and enjoying her food with a full appetite. Even after some bleeding began again in early January, we were confident that Chinese herbs could stop it as it appeared they had done when Gundi had been weak last June. Her fourth batch of herbs prescribed by Dr. Yuan included cuttlefish, oyster shell, charcoal, bark, roots, seeds and leaves. Hania provided a mix of belladonna, arnica, sequoia, juniper, plus *ferrum phosphoricum*. She believed parasites had returned. Gastroenterologist Dr. Chow's secretary had advised Gundi to go back onto the prescribed dose of anti-inflammatory drugs, which Gundi had reduced then stopped taking altogether at the beginning of December. Dr. Chow saw it as a maintenance program to prevent recurrence of inflammation. Gundi started on it again at the end of January.

This year's trip to the show in Philadelphia proved exhausting for Gundi. During the show she needed afternoon naps each day, and we had to buy simple foods at the market and minimize restaurant meals. She called her naturopath on our way back home and was lucky enough to get an appointment for the next day thanks to a late cancellation. Hania said her immune system, intestines and circulation were all compromised, so we returned home with a new batch of treatments. Gundi's iron levels were actually good and a lot of areas showed signs of improvement. Food-by-food analysis revealed what Gundi could and couldn't eat and take. Anti-inflammatory drugs were cut from eight to four daily, and multi-vitamins, probiotics and lactose cut out, although colostrum and yogurt were deemed okay. Hania said yes to white bread, cheese, honey, green tea, cooked vegetables, poached fruit, white rice, fish, ginger and even a glass of red wine daily; no to red meat, whole grains, nuts, garlic, spice, black tea, coffee and raw fruits and vegetables, even bananas. With this new regime and lots of rest over the next couple of weeks, Gundi gradually got better. Her bowel movements returned to normal, but tiredness lingered, enhanced by a deep bronchial cough followed by streaming cold, for which she used peppermint, thyme, hyssop, ginger, lemon, manuka honey and aloe vera juice.

This overall health shock spurred us to take control of our choices. We woke up to the fact that in order to get healthy, stay healthy and fend off disease, we needed to be much more proactive. We had always assumed our natural bodily immunity would stand us in good stead. Conventional medical treatments helped in emergency situations but then stalled a recovery, as all pharmaceutical medications—especially the powerful anti-inflammatory steroids—came with debilitating side effects. It became clear to us that we needed to take charge of body, mind, diet and our whole lifestyle by bringing everything back into balance using natural, or complementary, treatments to achieve lasting good health. While we were fortunate to reap the benefits of this country's imperfect universal health-care system, a more collaborative approach between different medical disciplines, both conventional and complementary, would secure far greater health outcomes than the current mutually exclusive approaches achieve in isolation. The health-care system needs to be more open to and to provide far better coverage for many complementary treatments.

A choice of treatments should be open to each individual, not restricted by commercial interests.

※ ※

At the start-up of the Toronto Brick Works Farmers Market in June, it was a bumper season for market produce, especially arugula and salad mixes. Sales for the co-op more than doubled, as we had hoped they would. I didn't have the capacity, or the will, to grow for any customers beyond the two Toronto farmers markets plus Victoria Inn and Oak Heights Winery. Managing the two markets was mostly tiring but thrilling too. It felt so good to be in demand, especially from such an enthusiastic and appreciative buying public. Help this year came from Georgia from England and Dana from nearby Whitby from the end of May to early August. They were both really helpful at markets, and Georgia a dab hand with the blackboard price list. In tandem, they worked fairly well in the garden, though they were slow at times. Over the summer, I also made the acquaintance of Peter Southward. He and I made a motivated team at both markets, and we thoroughly enjoyed the time and our success, consistently bringing home very healthy returns. There was minimal waste.

On market days the Quinte Organic stand would look plentiful and appealing. It was piled high with a large variety of fresh local certified organic items. Short-season specialties like heritage asparagus, rhubarb, snow peas, strawberries, lavender, heirloom tomatoes, sweet potatoes and sunchokes sat proudly alongside staples such as lettuce; beets; carrots; potatoes; garlic; a number of prewashed, ready-to-eat salad greens and mixes; green, yellow and purple beans; fresh lamb; and beef steaks, except nothing sat for long. Our co-operative of farmers had tapped into the ravenous appetite of sophisticated city consumers and chefs who craved the freshness, flavour and nutritional value of everything on offer. They were here because they were not blinded by supermarket Big Organic, with its flown-in Chinese garlic and year-round spring mix from mega-farms authorized to be rinsed in a chlorine bath, gassed to survive the long haul and trucked all the way from California. With us, our customers could be assured that the farmers cared enough about the way their food was produced to stand behind it and discuss its nature and freshness directly with them at market. It was as much about communication and education as it was about selling.

Selling the fruits of my labour at outdoor farmers markets has always been always a thrill. It never ceased to amaze how sought after our fresh organic produce was. It really shouldn't have been a wonder, as I explained how the spicy greens were picked that very morning and would last a good week or two in the fridge, if allowed to. And as the prospective customer savoured a sample, I warned "It really *is* spicy. Just wait a couple of seconds." They'd respond, "Oh, wow, that is *spi-cy*!" One enamoured returning customer asked what soil the salad mix had been grown in. When I told her a sandy loamy glacial till full of minerals, she said, "I knew it; I could taste it." That was gratifying, as were all the other compliments and thanks, and the extraordinary tally at the end of the day, when, once again, we were completely sold out.

Temagami

Every year as summer ebbs into the memory and fall is in full flow, it feels good to get a break from our civilized world. It is my time to recover my flagging energy and truly connect with nature and the wild. In Temagami, after a long day's paddle across large lakes and along narrow rivers, the reward was to discover an ideal island at which to set up camp. A waterfall roared off in the mid-distance, beyond the bend. The sun was going down as we gathered wood for the evening's campfire. Dusk was magic hour as our canoe drew us past ancient rock faces.

We had been guided into this old-growth sanctuary by ravens, and now loons announced their welcome. At this season of change marked by the onset of cold nights, the odd shower or flurry, gusty winds and the continued shedding of foliage, there were likely no other humans in our midst, but deer and bears, beavers, fish, frogs, ducks and birds were present. To share time and space with them was to feel a definite spiritual affinity to the wild and to those who have trodden these paths, paddled these waters before us.

Temagami old-growth forest at dawn (Photo by David Acomba)

At dawn a cluster of pines stood sentinel over the misted lake. A stroll revealed the island to us. Pink rocks were partly cloaked in moss and lichens, partly bare but drenched in early morning moisture. The sun suddenly pierced through the trees across the lake. The ground between the towering white pines and clumps of birch was soft with decomposing matter.

I try to make nature part of my every day, but there is no substitute for raw exposure to the wilds and the elements. Temagami transported us into a magical realm where the cycle of life and the vision of death were seen stark and true. Seeds germinate, struggle for survival. Plants live long, age gracefully, and finally return to the earth, embraced by the living forest floor which nurtures the cradling soil for a successor seed blowing in on the wind. Plants, wildlife and weather perform an absorbing, never-ending play, in which we were incidental participants rather than masters. We soaked up the charged energy; Nature challenged us and rewarded us with fleeting wonder and visions of great beauty.

Native peoples endured the extended cold of long winters out here in the woods because they respected nature, embraced it and gave thanks to it. They were part of it, and it became them. The blowing snows, the numbing cold, the evolving climate are a reminder how intimately connected we all are to earth, and how we meddle with it at our peril. As a civilization, we are accelerating the extinction of species; releasing toxins into the air, water and soil; effecting a changing climate; practicing irresponsible resource exploitation; displaying unfettered corporate greed.

As evolved human beings, we should be preserving every wild place, setting them aside for future generations. Our wide-eyed wonder is the key to our spirit, and our intimacy with nature in the wild enables us to affirm all life.

The self-willed forms of wild nature can call out fresh correspondences of spirit in a person. Wildness, in Coleridge's account, is an energy which blows through one's being, causing the self to shift into new patterns, opening up alternative perceptions of life. (Robert Macfarlane, *The Wild Places*)

9

Hoop Houses

2008

In September, we had purchased our first hoop house from Multi-Shelter Solutions. Earth mover Jack and crew excavated many truckloads of gravel from the pit abutting our property (with permission from the neighbours) and used it as base for the greenhouse and for the entire length of the laneway. The greenhouse kit arrived in October, and David and I put up the frame in November. We also set in the four concrete-block raised beds and had them filled with the excavated topsoil. The early freeze delayed completion, and it wasn't until the beginning of January, on a rare sunny and still day of minus 20 °C (minus 5 °F) that we got to putting the plastic cover on. Bob Porter helped us with the framing, finishing and covering.

On January 8, the temperature soared to 12 °C (55 °F) and the snow was all but gone. Time to start planting? Not quite. On January 9 came the first big test—wicked gusts from the tail end of a cold front moving through. All day the winds blew, and they ripped out the plastic under one batten around the hoop-house door at the east end. I patched it up. Unfortunately, the extreme cold when we attached the plastic cover and quick change to much milder temperatures had caused the plastic to stretch and become loose. We would adjust it in springtime when it got up over 10 ºC (50 ºF). The temperature in the hoop house was a few degrees warmer than outside, and positively balmy on sunny days. Let the planning for seeding begin!

※　※

The supermarkets were full of produce, most of it having been treated to withstand the rigours of travelling large distances to get that far. Global food prices were continuing their upward spiral driven by speculative commodities markets here in the Western world. This was proving disastrous to the poor and hungry in the developing world, and prices here were bound to rise with the escalating price of oil. Growers of food would feel the pinch as transportation costs continued to skyrocket, while speculators drive prices further upward, providing a boon to the dealmakers and middlemen in the distribution chain.

How could we consumers counter this inexorable trend? The best way was to shop close to home and choose an alternative regional food supply and distribution system that was a lot more sustainable than the mainstream corporate multinational food-trading system which was mightily wasteful and controlled by big players. Farmers had to opt out of what Gavin Dandy of Everdale Environmental Learning Centre called "that tired old global food commodity game: they grow lots of a few crops and sell them at bargain basement prices to big buyers who then send them on down the line of middlemen, wholesalers, distributors, processors, packers and retailers. All of this mass-produced food gets pooled and swapped and generally denuded of goodness until you can't tell where it came from or how it was grown." Tainted food scandals were on the rise; no surprise, this, when industrial food products have such a long, convoluted route through a slew of handlers from source to our plate.

An alternative came from family, small-scale farms that were already growing food organically and caring for the land, soil, plants, birds and bees and other insects in order to preserve and enhance the whole farm environment for future farmers to tend. There was demand for more of them practicing their craft whole-heartedly, without shortcuts. Farmers could select heirloom varieties and untreated seeds, thereby passing on the diversity, variety and flavour that our ancestors grew and ate. These farmers (who now had to have their products annually inspected and verified in order to legitimately label them "organic") then had the opportunity to sell their food direct to the public through local and regional farmers markets that were filling out our cityscapes and townscapes, and to hungry restaurants and chefs, natural food stores, progressive school boards, even forward-thinking hospitals and businesses. Or, they could sell community shared agriculture (CSA) food shares and so supply the local community, neighbours, friends and fresh food aficionados. The markets were there and the consumer was leading the way. Smallholders, homesteaders, hobby farmers too should have been allowed to take their eggs, dairy and chickens to market as they had done traditionally, without the increasingly stifling restrictions mandated by meddling governments and threatened marketing boards. People should have received every encouragement and incentive to grow food, preserve food and buy it in their locality from farmers who truly care about freshness, flavour, variety and the welfare of the animals they manage, the natural environment and the land on which their food is produced.

In the interest of transparency, if conventional farmers continued to use genetically modified and chemically treated seeds and chemical fertilizers, pesticides, herbicides and sewage sludge in their food production, they should have been made to tell us. If food was safe to eat, why were certain added ingredients kept secret? If some ingredients were not safe to eat, what were they doing in our food in the first place? Shouldn't we have the choice not to eat them, based on our knowledge of what's in them?

In southern Ontario, there had been significant progress in recent years toward building a regional sustainable food-distribution system, a network of farmers markets, organic farmers, schools. The Greater Toronto area was well on its way to becoming one of North America's largest clusters for food and farming. The 100-mile-diet and buy-local programs were helping to raise awareness among consumers and to encourage ethical purchasing and growing of food. However, it was important that consumers and purveyors of food alike continue supporting fair-trade initiatives and small-scale and organic growers of exotics like coffee, cocoa, tea, tropical fruits, olive oil, wines, beers and specialty packaged products from around the world.

Local small-scale farmers, employing organic methods, needed to bring fresh food to market or have the customer come to the farm. In our communities—be they cities, towns, villages, counties, or regions—people needed to know of the goodness, vitality and value of fresh, local, organic food. We farmers had to first catch up with, then be slightly ahead of demand so that we could supply innovative food purveyors, such as restaurants and natural food stores, and also the general public at farmers markets. In-season, freshly harvested foods were clearly best, but in the off-season, we could provide preserved goodness in the form of root vegetables, pickles, preserves, oils, vinegars and fermented vegetables. Some farmers toiled year-round with production and sales without a pause for air. I was one farmer who chose to take a break each winter, plan ahead, network, read, research, write, travel, play, rest, spend more time with family and friends and recharge to ready for the next season.

※ ※

Gundi's health was pretty much back to normal. She was energetic, working hard, eating and drinking normally, looking radiant. Her illness seemed already to have happened a long time ago. The time since had been challenging for us as a couple and for the farm. Rolling Hills Organics was in its fourth year as member of Quinte Organic Farmers Co-operative, and we had done very well by it, increasing revenues substantially year over year, thanks mostly to the success of two Toronto farmers markets. In hindsight, the co-op helped by paying our mileage and time but detracted from sales by the cut it took. All the phone calls, meetings, planning, reporting, accounting and mollycoddling it required and, more particularly, the petty and personal ill feelings and envy it generated made some of us decide to run through the season then quit. Peter Southward and I had by this time cemented an enjoyable camaraderie, but our enthusiasm and drive were often undermined by a gnawing negative attitude toward us. At the markets we generated bumper sales; Riverdale and Brick Works provided us with a banner year. Rolling Hills Organics could still not keep up with the demand for our premium prewashed, ready-to-eat salad greens, which included several mixes and the perennially popular arugula. Baby carrots, beets and fresh herbs all sold well. Christina Temple, who had started out as a customer of the co-op, opened up sales for our farm through her to a few select restaurants, Mistura, Opus, Boba and Citizen among them. With a few small bumps along the way, which largely related to packaging and delivery issues, we initially passed the restaurants' stringent quality control and then steadily developed a stellar reputation. The chefs were prepared to pay a price that was comparable to market retail. And they too wanted more. It was a delicate exercise to divide produce among the farmers markets, Toronto restaurants, local Northumberland restaurants and specialty food stores. I continued to deliver weekly to Oak Heights Winery and the Victoria Inn. Also on board came Local Infusion and the 100-Mile Diner in Warkworth. Sales to Toronto restaurants were destined to expand, and Rolling Hills Organics and Peter Southward's Trentview Farm would have a combined stand at Riverdale and Brick Works. For us, the co-op was history. Independence would enable our own farms to retain the full retail price, and the high demand we anticipated meant that we would be able to increase prices slightly as long as we maintained our high quality standards.

The growing season was fun and hard work. The new hoop house was a challenge early in the season. Seed starts had a longer lead time than I anticipated in their unheated environment, and I found it hard to regulate temperatures and watering. Early sun in March and April was too intense and the ventilation too sparse. The soil was deficient in organic matter, and I failed to water the beds sufficiently. Salad greens shot up but quickly gave up the ghost, looking pale and spindly. They didn't bother with a second or third growth after the first cutting. So it was that our main helper for the season, the zealous Tracey from Ottawa, and I changed the soil in August, clearing out the dry beds and refilling them with a layer of hay and barrowloads of topsoil blended with organic sheep manure. This mix provided much improved harvests of arugula and salad mixes from September to late November. Then came the early cold, which sharply closed production down for the season.

Barefoot Tracey was a brick through the summer, braving the frequent winds and rains. Together we marvelled at the ever-changing storm cloud formations, huge hammerheads rumbling across the sky, mutating wondrous blue-sky windows. Her salad-green washing with Gundi was indispensable, this chore having become a major operation ahead of each market day. Tracey loved doing the markets and her thoroughness and outgoing nature were helpful and refreshing. She also helped Gundi with meals and invented her own. I was sorry to see her go in mid-August. Local Vicky helped with the early rounds of weeding before succumbing to the sun and rains.

In late September we picked apples. We hauled in a bumper crop on an amazing crisp bright day of blue skies, sunshine and kisses blown by Pomona, the glowing goddess of the gardens. We filled a tractor loader plus pails of apples green, yellow, pink, striped, large and small and strained them through our lovely hand-cranked wooden apple press from Harmony Valley, Ohio. The tangy, complex taste of several very different older varieties, the delectable Duchess among them, was alive. The liquid was bottled, with lots going into the freezer for a midwinter burst of preserved summer freshness.

> *It has to do with the earth. The human woman gives birth just as the earth gives birth to the plants ... so woman magic and earth magic are the same. They are related. And the personification of the energy that gives birth to forms and nourishes forms is properly female. It is in the agricultural world of ancient Mesopotamia, the Egyptian Nile, and in the earlier planting-culture systems that the Goddess is the dominant mythic form.* (Joseph Campbell)

In Inca mythology, Mama Pacha or Pachamama is a fertility goddess who presides over planting and harvesting. She causes earthquakes. Since Pachamama is a "good mother," people usually toast to her honor before every meeting or festivity, in some regions by spilling a small amount of *chicha* on the floor before drinking the rest. This toast is called *challa* and it is made almost every day.

Many neo-Pagans actively worship Gaia. Beliefs regarding Gaia vary, ranging from the common Wiccan belief that Gaia is earth (or in some cases, the spiritual embodiment of earth, or the goddess of earth), to the broader neo-Pagan belief that Gaia is the goddess of all creation, a mother goddess from which all other gods spring. Gaia is sometimes thought to embody all the planets in the solar system, and sometimes even the entire universe.

Gundi's visit from a black bear in our own garden, at her very door, excited her beyond measure. On a hot early afternoon at the end of August, he came sniffing around. Bears stock up on reserves at this time of year, needing to gain 12 kilos (25 pounds) per week to prepare them for winter. Sweet corn and apples are high on their wanted list, hence this one's visit. A handsome, mellow fellow, he was civil enough, even returning when prompted and posing for a photograph on his hind legs. Bees love apples too, as well as buckwheat and any source of nectar. In late summer, the monarch butterflies feast on milkweed before their long flight south over land and ocean to the forests of Michoacan in Mexico. Birds busy themselves for winter, some for a long trip south, some just to stock up.

We have loved to watch the birds feed on the sunflower seeds we put out for them year-round. Some said we shouldn't feed them year-round, as it spoiled them and interfered with their migration patterns and attracted squirrels, raccoons, skunks and even bears. We did it anyway. At the feeders on the deck and in the fields beyond, we witnessed an astounding array of birds: the purple finch, goldfinch, blue jay, crow, raven, purple martin, tree swallow, barn swallow, black-capped chickadee, white-breasted nuthatch, house wren, eastern bluebird, wood thrush, American robin, European starling, cedar waxwing, house sparrow, dark-eyed junco, northern cardinal, indigo bunting, red-winged blackbird, bobolink, common grackle, Baltimore oriole, evening grosbeak, rose-breasted grosbeak, red-headed woodpecker, red-bellied woodpecker, downy woodpecker, pileated woodpecker, yellow-bellied sapsucker, great blue heron, turkey vulture, Canada goose, red-tailed hawk, ring-necked pheasant, ruffed grouse, wild turkey, killdeer, herring gull, rock dove, mourning dove, great horned owl, ruby-throated hummingbird …

A less happy encounter with wildlife happened one evening in November when our friend Dorothy, driving home from Peterborough with Gundi as passenger, smacked into a large buck deer that materialized from the twilight. Poor deer, poor car, poor girls! The investigating policeman noted that there was always a spate of collisions with deer at this time of year, just after the end of hunting season. The siege lifted, the unfortunate creatures come out of the bush to feed, and smack! The policeman dispatched the killing bullet, and an alert passing motorist got to bag the fresh carcass. We were left to bemoan the ever-increasing rarity of deer sightings.

2009

Helpers Meredith and Fred asked Gundi if she minded if they sang while weeding the fields with her. Absolutely not! What greater expression of engagement and communion could there be? Conversely, Megan and Roberta, both from Peterborough, conspired to bring their participation on the farm to a grinding halt. It was a horribly cold and wet spring, and the greens took an age to gain a foothold. (It was August before the arugula and mixed greens came into their own.) After being entrusted with seeding most of the vegetables—the first time ever that I relinquished this precious task—the two girls grew restless after Megan was granted leave for a vacation to the Caribbean. After a day of acrimony on her return, I told Gundi the girls were not happy. "Get rid of them," she said unequivocally. And so they were gone. Gundi herself stepped into the breach, as demand for her glass sculptures had plummeted with the general economy south of the border tanking. Our first trip to Baltimore for a combined wholesale and retail show in February had been an unmitigated disaster, and, fittingly perhaps, we very nearly slid into a truck and were off on the icy way home.

Young Mia from Warkworth helped Gundi with the washing and packaging of salad greens. This procedure now took up several hours three days a week because we served Riverdale and Brick Works farmers markets along with several local restaurants. New on board this year were Zest and the Northside. Chef Ray at Zest was refreshingly enthusiastic but very particular, making the quantity of produce to deliver hard to gauge. On the other hand, Johnny at the Northside was the epitomize of cool and carefree, and he lapped up whatever came. When we tried lunch at Zest, I was taken aback to find that my sandwich was served with floppy, tasteless arugula, definitely *not* from our farm, though I had delivered some. A celebratory dinner at the Northside was fabulous, even though they had sold out of our greens.

Rolling Hills and Trentview had parted company with Quinte Organic over the winter as planned. Peter and I relished our new freedom and had fun at every market. Sales were up despite the recession, and our main problem was producing sufficient volume. It became embarrassing to promise eager salad eaters they'd have their greens next week every week through May, June and July. The arugula and mustards just sat there in the cool soil and sulked. The weeds grew, of course, and crowded out the good guys, so undersupply at the increasingly competitive markets was the norm. I neglected Toronto restaurants in favour of the generally upbeat customers of my Thursday delivery route. Sadly, Peter and Phyllis at Oak Heights Winery were gone from one day to the next, and new chef Richard did not share Peter's gusto. With his increased responsibility, Jeff at Victoria Inn urged more of the same.

Toronto's Riverdale Farmers Market was generally slower than before, especially early and late in the season and on days with poor weather, but we usually left early, sold out as usual. Brick Works was vibrant all season despite the dusty, noisy demolition and new construction all around. We continued to set up outside in most weathers, teeming rain and blowing storms being the exception. We were rewarded by some exceptionally faithful regular customers who plonked down surprising amounts of money every time. Thank you, Mike, Ned, Murray, Kathy, Ava, Shakir. New products this year included pestos made with garlic scapes, arugula, sweet basil and sun-dried tomatoes; basil- and cilantro-infused oils; and rosemary apple cider vinegar. For the next year, we planned to reintroduce the herbal teas, as our customers missed them. Double sunflowers made a splash in September, just after the arugula finally came to life. A break for niece Mieke's wedding to Martin in Berlin had given the garden time to replenish itself, and the brief burst of heat helped enormously.

October was time to restock with garlic, so I met Ken Best at Best Berry Farm just south of Norwood. We took 75 pounds of very robust hardneck musics and planted them around Thanksgiving. I was very organized this year putting the garden to bed, plowing residues under and straw-mulching the garlic and some of the lavender. Jack came to grade a flat topsoil base for a second hoop house, and he took away my cherished but dormant Massey 35 red tractor in exchange. He was just back from his annual two-week hunting trip, spent with 20 or so other testosterone-pumped males in the woods up north.

"How was hunting?" I asked.

"Terrible," he replied. "No deer at all; just coyotes all around."

"Good," I said.

He looked at me scornfully and, after a pause for thought, he passed his judgment. "I bet you don't even have a gun, do you?"

David and I built the frame and erected the hoops, and Bob and Howard helped to attach the plastic. Then, hey presto, a new hoop house, another thousand square feet in which to plant early-season greens to better cater to demand from restaurants in April and May and farmers markets until the field crops come on in mid-June.

Mum's passing

My dear old mum passed away in her sleep four days after suffering a major stroke in Shrewsbury in mid-December. A lone deer wandering across the snow in the low cold sun of a winter morn was a precursor to her departure. Then the winter solstice—a time of transition in the annual struggle between light and darkness, warmth and cold, abundance and shortage, life and death—was upon us, and with it communion with friends followed by an exquisite morning snow rainbow around a sparkling cascade of crystals. On my return home after Mum's life remembrance in Shrewsbury in early January, again a lone deer wandered away across the morning snow. As Mum departed her life on earth, her eldest granddaughter, Mieke, was expecting her first child, to be named Emilia. She would have been Mum's first great-grandchild.

As my dear friend Cornelia remarked, when the time comes that both parents are gone, one is suddenly, starkly an orphan. Gone with their passing is the facility to be a child, and this is a sad and scary moment. Gundi had lost her mother, who was the grand age of 95, a few months before, in April. When Mum passed away eight months later, I realized I was on my own, an adult deprived of his mother's unconditional love. Although I was blessed to have the love of my wife, close family and friends, I was now bereft of both my true nurturers, and it hurt. Without children of our own, we orphaned ones often have nothing to project our love onto except each other. As human beings, we are, however, incredibly resilient, and love finds a way to get spread around, especially within families and between friends. In fact, it becomes reinvigorated at key times in our lives—weddings and funerals, births and deaths, for example.

On a Severn riverside walk in Shrewsbury just before we met to remember Mum's life, I was liberated by an overwhelming feeling of Mum's spirit and presence. "Go on, off you go; live your life. I've done all I can and can't take in anymore. You're on your own now," her voice told me. The next day was bright, frosty and cold. Up on Haughmond Hill, we watched the dazzling sun set over Shrewsbury and the surrounding snowy hills and mountains. Darkness descended. *Bye-bye, dear Mum.*

10

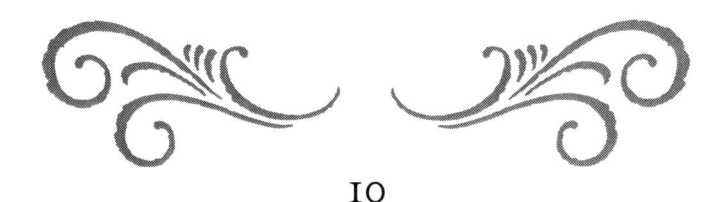

Into a Second Decade

Value is not made of money, but a tender balance of expectation and longing. (Barbara Kingsolver, *Animal, Vegetable, Miracle*)

It seemed such a critical watershed time, but this was maybe because the world was speeding up, I was slowing down, and time was becoming more precious. Two recent studies had predicted that within 50 years, climate change would send economies into sharp decline and that in the same time frame, fish as food would disappear from the oceans and the polar ice caps would melt. (Both were already doing so at an alarmingly accelerated rate). How reckless could we be as environmental regulators and planetary managers? Despite the writing on the wall of dire comeuppances, the powerful elite was turning the other cheek and pressing on regardless with their ruthless plunder.

Few people anywhere were coming through the latest debt spiral and global financial and food crises unscathed. It all stemmed from many years of unfettered greed on the part of a few. Payback time. It was affecting the obscenely rich fat cats and top dogs, the merely affluent, the well-to-do, the desperately coping, the down on their luck and, most extremely, the growing numbers of poor and malnourished. In jeopardy were lives, ways of life, livelihoods, small businesses, large corporations, whole industries, even governments and nations. The general reaction was to hunker down to weather the storm, as if this were a passing tempest that would rage for a while then blow itself out, for the sun to rise again tomorrow as it always had. But would it rise in quite the same way? There was boom and bust but no echo. It was a frenzied scramble for stability and comfort and more and more innocent, frugal citizens were being trampled. Instead of conserving dwindling natural resources, investing in infrastructure and making a transformational switch to renewables, as common intelligence should tell us was the expedient thing to do, there was a piranha-like feeding frenzy to get at the existing spoils as rapidly and as profitably as possible. There seemed to be no limit to the brazen greed, stupidity and short-sightedness. It was (and is) suicidal pathological behaviour.

Leaders of developed nations' economies were digging a deeper hole, printing obscene amounts of money (billions, even trillions), propping up ailing concerns, reinforcing bankrupt institutions, bailing out gluttonous banks and bankers that resisted regulation. In the process, the struggling economies of increasingly debt-ridden nations were squeezed and coerced into taking on yet more debt. Cultural decadence led governments in cahoots with the bankers to take their desperation out on the general populace by demanding extreme austerity as a cure for a disease of their creation. Despite the noble efforts of many people, we were paralyzed as a society by that tragedy of the commons—inertia—unable to change fundamentally misguided thinking and principles. Controlling interests made quick fixes with cosmetic plugs of gaping holes in our governance, ignoring corporate crime and corruption and all the time backsliding on promises, commitments and treaties and turning their backs on the future. Sad to say, this is apparently our ordained collective nature. Valuable contributions by transforming individual thinkers and doers and activist movements all gave momentum to a semblance of counter-flow, but tragically, without a critical mass, they could not reverse the path, which we seem to be stuck on at present, to dystopia that George Orwell (in *1984* and *Animal Farm*) and Aldous Huxley (in *Brave New World*) had warned us about.

We show a stubborn resistance to fundamental change, although we are delivered daily ever more evidence that we need to adapt or continue sliding into decline. Denial and abdication of responsibility are at the heart of the paralysis, as is a sad lack of overarching vision and leadership. The message of hope and promise of change brought by Barack Obama on his election as President of the United States largely evaporated over time into thin air. His sparkling oratory could not mask the fact that, as William Pitt the Elder, British Prime Minister from 1766 to 1778, warned in a 1770 speech to the House of Lords, "Unlimited power is apt to corrupt the minds of those who possess it". On issues like GMOs, secret prisons, banker bailouts, due process and marijuana use, campaign promises were not to be met. Such a waste! The best hope for redemption at this juncture remained the activism of grassroots movements together with the drive of brave, outspoken whistleblowers and the dedication of committed community clusters.

Twenty-first century society likes to pride itself on being civilized. To look around the world today at the exploitation, abuse, inequality and geopolitical conflict is to see scant justification for this. Many hunter-gatherers and indigenous tribes and peoples were better adapted than most cultures today to relating to each other, cooperating, living frugally within their means, wasting little and in living sustainably in harmony with nature.

Call it naïve thinking by all means, but not because I espouse peaceful resolutions, ends to conflicts and cooperative solutions but because I have had a measure of misplaced faith in corrupt institutions and practices. Government-sanctioned savings plans, bank loans, credit cards, mortgages, exorbitant interest rates, phony investment rackets, Ponzi schemes with global reach, hedge funds, housing bubbles, the stock market, derivatives, rehypothecation—enough already! How they have manipulated us and tied us up in knots. There are more ethical ways to do business and to trade sensibly and sustainably. Microfinancing, Slow Money, downsizing, living with minimal debt and simply investing in ourselves and our localities are increasingly appealing alternatives. It has to be unforgiveable for governments to continue to bail out the banks, allow corporate directors to receive obscene bonus payments, borrow from tomorrow and the planet and live beyond their means, all without confronting spiralling debts. Failure to rein in debt leaves the threat of an out-of-control future which may even be more imminent than some have predicted.

In the wake of destructive developments in the world at large, it was tempting to run and hide. In spite of breathing in fresh country air and eating fresh organic fruits of the land, the modern cocktail of environmental and radiation hazards and toxins meant that it was vital to work overtime to maintain body, mind and soul in good shape. The recent stresses of Dad's and then Mum's passing from this world, Gundi's serious illness and ongoing pressures to make a living at the things I cared for all took their toll. It was clear that my body could not continue to cope with the physical exertions of farming forever. And so it was important to take heed of what was happening both in our small world and in the large one out beyond the horizon. Vigilance, adjustments and actions were called for constantly.

Our years up here high in the hills have taught me to focus my energies on what we can do to live well and to recognize the importance of living up to even a small amount of our potential. When we have this luxury of choosing how and where we live, let's seize the opportunity! It is surely a moral imperative for those with insight and foresight to seek out and grab meaningful livelihoods by the horns, to pursue those things vital to our individual and collective well-being: honesty, integrity, understanding, forgiveness, intuition, will, passion, direction, imagination, humanity, morality, caring, empathy, resilience, resistance, independence, liberty, evolution, trust, love, education, healing, creation and cultivation—all that elevates us as human beings and enhances life on earth. Forget shock and awe, pre-emptive strikes, the big-stick approach, extreme capitalism, global expansionism. Common sense, hard work, loving care, community building and living within our means are traditional values well worth dusting off. In working together for mutual goals to turn the tide against rampant greed, aggression and mean-spiritedness, we do our small part in fostering truth, honesty and peace, and we stand up to the narrow interests of the elite few.

Rise like lions after slumber
In unvanquishable number,
Shake your chains to earth like dew
Which in sleep had fall'n on you.
Ye are many, they are few.
(Percy Bysshe Shelley, from "The Mask of Anarchy")

2010

As we headed into winter, I read the article "Solar Power Opportunities for Rural Ontario" in a local newspaper. *Hmm, sounds interesting.* A solar power developer was seeking landowners with about an acre of sunlit open property. The field up the hill was ideal, alongside the five acres that we had reforested four years ago. Landowners were being offered annual payments equal to 10 percent of the gross revenue of the project and were not responsible for any costs, investment, property taxes, maintenance or liabilities. This all sounded in line with what we had always wanted: to utilize renewable energy sources without putting up a large capital investment. What had changed? Ontario's new Green Energy Act was allowing renewable energy developers to enter the field, make the capital investment and partner with landowners by leasing land for their projects. Participating in phasing out extreme dependence on coal and nuclear technologies for electricity and contributing to local community supply of renewable power was something we were eager to do. We duly signed up for the first array of solar panels to be installed in a pastured field up the hill. We leased a whole acre to a Canadian solar energy company and were excited to be on the cusp of generating electricity both to go straight into the local grid and to provide supplementary income for the farm.

We had always been envious of Jack and Kevin, who had purchased a lovely piece of land with another couple, Kim and Roberto. It had sweeping views in every direction. They built a wonderful straw-bale house atop their hill that we could see as we looked east from the high point on our land. They were off the grid, relying on an array of solar panels and a small wind turbine as independent power sources. When two windstorms in close succession had cut off our power for two to three days, they were able to carry on as normal. With wood heat, a propane gas stove and a dug well, we were able to get by with heat, cooked food and water. But, during such power outages, it was not possible to cool, freeze or light, use the drilled well with its submersible pump, or connect with the outside world. We wanted our own solar panels and small-scale wind turbine. If only we could be part of a visionary community, owning our own endlessly renewable energy source with zero-sum fossil-fuel emissions, as have sprung up in Europe. Forward-thinking rural communities have shown it can be done with sufficient willpower and organization. Pairs of concrete-mounted solar tracking panels had sprung up all over the hills around us, mostly on the edges of farmers' fields. They took up little space and were harnessing energy from the sun, of which we are blessed with good amounts year-round, even through those long winter months. They also generated new heaven-sent income for farmers and landowners. We waited and waited for our own to be approved, installed and hooked up to the grid, only to be told again and again that the Ontario Power Authority faced local constraints and didn't have enough capacity to connect us with even micropanels, as they needed to upgrade their system first.

It was frustrating to hear the not-in-my-back-yard resistance to wind turbines. Local sentiment was often vehemently opposed to them as residents railed against perceived health risks. Tilting at windmills. *Plus ça change, plus c'est la même chose.* I did, and still do, agree with the rejection of mega-projects and *industrial-scale* multiturbine installations in the line of sight and within earshot of rural residents, but there needed to be accommodation for *small-scale* generation of wind power, with setbacks of reasonable distances to protect neighbours, using small turbines on residential lots and larger ones on farms and large acreages, just as there was room for appropriate-scale solar power generation. From my perspective, the implementation of harnessing ever more clean, harmless, abundant energy naturally emitted by the sun and the wind needs to be a priority, though the massive scale of some projects should be reserved for expansive land- and seascapes, well away from where people live, work, rest and play. Each project to generate renewable power is a step toward directly reducing dependence on nuclear energy and on fossil fuels like coal and gas, which continue to exacerbate climate change through their greenhouse gas emissions. Progressive communities large and small, and even entire nations like Denmark and Germany, have rolled out wind- and solar-energy projects and are currently reaping the rewards of their foresight, so why not follow suit here in Ontario with our vast open terrain and abundance of sun and wind? The problem here has been the poor politics of introducing a new top-down provincial energy program with scant respect for the rights of citizens and communities. While the province is looking to spend billions of dollars on new nuclear installations (subject to further debilitating cost overruns), there is already a ready alternative of spending on infrastructure to accelerate development of renewable energies.

The Institute of Science in Society wrote in its 2009 report *Green Energies, 100% Renewables by 2050*:

> Wind energy alone can supply 40 times the world's electricity or 5 times its total energy consumption. PV technologies are improving by leaps and bounds, and electricity from solar panels is already as cheap as electricity from the grid. Bio-gas from wastes has transformed rural China, and waste-incinerating community cookers are poised to do the same in Africa. Air condition and energy from deep water, saline agriculture for food and fuel, and estuarine reef for tapping tidal energy are further options in addition to well established micro-hydroelectric and geothermal energies.

Promising developments on the horizon include thermo-electrics for recycling waste heat into electricity, artificial photosynthesis for harvesting and storing solar energy, and the potential for solving our nuclear waste problem by low temperature transmutation.

These are exciting times. All we need to save the planet is for our leaders to follow the way of nature and the will and wisdom of the people.

With a cool wet spring followed by a mediocre summer of only rare heat, 2009 had been a trying year. From the very get-go, this new one was a bumper year for us on the farm. After an exceptionally mild winter with very little snow, spring blew in early. As assistant Natalia, who now lives with her family in Scotland, noted, it was an incredibly fecund time, with early heat, blossoms full on the fruit trees, birds busy and abundant and seeds getting off to a fast start. The hoop houses seeded in mid-March were in full production by mid-April, and I was without ready markets for all the arugula, lettuce, salad mix, kale, chard and spinach until the first farmers market and the awakening of chefs to the novelty of local produce availability in mid-May. The previous year had frustrated by not yielding any decent harvest of our best-selling arugula until August; now we had plenty of the stuff from April right through to December and even early January.

Natalia helped me hit the ground running with weeks of hard graft and enthusiastic, wide-ranging dialogue as one glorious spring day followed the next. We planted, picked stones and weeded as the weeds grew in every bit as fecund as the plants. Grasses and sprouted grain from last year's straw mulch blanketed the beds and made early harvests a nightmare to prepare for market. Gundi and

Meredith—who, with her parents and husband Andrew, owns a nearby farm in Roseneath—formed a great team of salad washers, sifters, spinners, weighers and baggers, but how they groaned at each new bin of salad and grass in equal measure! We got through it, and Lukash from Warkworth braved the heat and the picky hand-weeding with no fuss. Perseverance paid off with a steady stream of fresh-picked prewashed greens, herbs, beets and carrots for two Toronto farmers markets, three Toronto restaurants, and five local restaurants every week from May through November.

All through the growing and market season the weather was ideal; a lovely warm spring with regular rainfall was followed by a hot summer and a warm fall likewise blessed with ideal moisture. This was the opportunity for our farm to step up to the plate for our first season selling solo. After four years with Quinte Organic Farmers Co-operative and a year in tandem with Trentview Farm, we set up at Riverdale and Brick Works farmers markets with Rolling Hills Organics signs. Over the winter Peter and Wendy had sold Trentview Farm and moved out to their new home on Prince Edward Island. This meant our stepping up production and taking over sales of Peter's grass-fed and grass-finished Dexter beef. Farmer John McGriskin kept the cattle at his farm in Omemee. From John, we would order a whole beef, cut by the butcher to our specifications, as required. Customers were grateful for the ongoing supply of prime steaks, roasts and ground and stewing beef, and we took on new converts through the year. We even had one couple, Keir and Jenn—vegetarians!—eager to try the beef. They had heard about the health benefits of grass-fed, grass-finished beef and reported back that they loved it. Our beef now became a monthly treat for them, and they claimed they still didn't eat meat, just our beef! Most popular cuts overall were the New York strip loins, rib-eyes, and lean ground.

Dexter cattle, originating from Ireland, are the smallest of the

European cattle breeds, being about half the size of a traditional Hereford and about one-third the size of a Friesian milking cow. They were considered a rare breed, but they are now considered a recovering breed. The mature Dexter cows weigh between 600 and 700 pounds, and mature bulls about 1,000 pounds. John's Dexters were grass-fed year-round on pasture and hay and were grass-finished. When evaluating the benefits of grass-fed beef, it is important to ensure that they are "finished" on grass, rather than grain, for the 90 to 160 days before slaughter. If cattle are finished on grain in this time, the levels of important nutrients like CLA and omega-3 decrease dramatically in the animal's tissues. The beef we took to market had all been from animals moved from pasture to pasture in the growing season and fed on good hay all winter. They were never kept in confinement. Shelter from the rain, wind and cold was always available, but they stayed in the fresh air in all seasons.

Our reward for the increased range and production was the unprecedented sales tally at the end of each market. Our customers went with gusto for the garlic scape, citrus basil, arugula and sun-dried tomato pestos created *con brio* by Gundi. They craved more of the tangy, thick-cut Seville orange marmalade we made over the winter. Our very own Northumberland Hills honey was added to the mix and was well-received. The six blends of herbal teas, each offering a different health benefit, found a very select audience. One day I had an amusing encounter with Warren, a regular customer at market, when he asked me what tea I recommended.

"Depends what you want it for. Relaxing, stimulating, cleansing, energizing? Digestion, decongestion?"

"I want to feel thirty years younger." He smiled.

"Here, this one, for vitality, says twenty years on the label," I joked.

"OK, I'll just take two teaspoons instead of one."

"Careful, don't overdo it; you might revert to childhood."

"Oh no, I couldn't bear to go through that again."

Several weeks later, I asked about the tea, and Warren said he was feeling great!

On the downside, the heirloom tomatoes grown in the hoop houses were not ventilated well enough and succumbed to leaf mould during a particularly hot and humid spell when I must have overwatered. Having pruned them way back and seen the blight continue to spread, I evacuated them all and determined never to grow them again, particularly since other growers had a spate of sundry beauties. The next year, it was to be spring and fall greens and herbs only in the hoop houses.

Christina Temple had been a loyal, regular customer at the farmers markets from the very first season in the city. She gave me great confidence as a grower, insisting that all the leafy greens and herbs we took to market were of premium quality, fresh, full of flavour and, most important for her, chock full of nutrition. She should know, as she had worked in the restaurant business for many years and understood its foibles, quirks and nuances well. In 1997, she had authored a best-selling book called *Beat Toronto: 50 of Our City's Most Interesting Restaurants*. Being aware of, procuring and eating nutritious food became central to maintaining her health. Some fifteen years before, in moving into a new apartment, Chris had been exposed to several environmental toxins in the building, including benzene, cadmium and toluene. From this she had developed a blood disease called myelodysplastic syndrome (MDS), a type of leukemia. Very early on, Chris had made the very brave decision to fight for her health mainly through natural diet and treatments. For her, this meant switching to eating organic food, drinking pure water from trusted sources and being extremely cautious in general about what passed her lips.

This meant no processed foods or refined salts, sugars or flour. She had to do this, as constant monitoring of her blood count and platelets revealed frequent alarming dips. Natural treatments included herbal supplements, body flushes, lymphatic drainage, sweat lodges, massage, regular exercise and yoga. Though her regime was often extremely hard over many years, Chris kept a bright smile, a readiness to laugh and a general zest for fun in life. All her determined efforts have brought Chris a long way in turning back the disease that has plagued her all these years. She has remained an enthusiastic advocate of certified organic produce, the fresher the better. Her body is incredibly sensitive to foods that are not organically grown; she can tell immediately if a carrot has been tainted by pesticides or if leafy greens are substandard or not local.

Troubled by her doctors' contention that Chris would probably have to live with her symptoms of low platelets for the rest of her life, I passed on to her a promising treatment which I urged her to try. It was a herbal dietary supplement synergistically formulated to promote healthy platelet counts and immune-system function for individuals who have imbalances associated with blood-platelet deficiencies. The doctors who had developed it believed that a more balanced and detoxified body has an increased potential to support healthy bone marrow function, thereby improving the quality and quantity of healthy blood platelets created and maintained in the body. Indications are that this natural herbal blend is working well for Chris, and long-term dedication to her self-realized overall health program is bringing positive results of elevated energy and a healthy appetite.

Peter and Chris serving a customer at Riverdale Farmers Market, Toronto

Chris was becoming ever more involved helping us all year at both markets, vouching for the flavour, nutritional value and freshness of all that we showcased. I have learned a great deal from her, and she has provided endless valuable suggestions of what to grow both for market and for innovative chefs always on the lookout for new angles and fresh varieties. Besides Chris's rapport with customers, her strong sales and her knowledge of the food and restaurant industries, we have a lot of fun working together. All the hard work and thorough planning gave us a great sense of achievement and satisfaction. Being outside preparing the ground, planting seeds, seeing plants grow, harvesting them at their peak, selling them that same day fresh, laughing and joking, receiving compliments from customers, coming home tired with a healthy financial return, sleeping like a baby… What else could a grower and seller ask for?

For several years Chris and I generally worked the markets together. We both loved the back-and-forth banter with customers, especially the regulars that chatted awhile. Unable to have children herself because of her health condition, Chris loves babies and little ones and would spontaneously rush up excitedly to unsuspecting mothers, engaging them in conversation and cooing at their little ones. Naturally, being childless too, I also love kids, but Chris has a way of befriending mothers that is quite disarming. Many customers have specific health concerns, of course, for themselves and their loved ones, so it was gratifying to share our combined knowledge, experiences and recommendations. To have new customers return the following week with glowing stories about their cooking adventures and purchases was a pleasant reward for our toils.

Chris remarked: "I am testament to the fact that we only live once, we are what we eat and we must live every day like it's our last; enjoy our friends, the moments we all share and love living life; both the good and the bad."

It was the irrepressible Elizabeth Harris who had given me my big break as a certified organic grower all those years ago. Then as vice-president of Quinte Organic Farmers Co-operative, I approached Elizabeth to apply for the co-op to be a vendor at her flagship organic farmers market at Riverdale Farm in Cabbagetown, Toronto. She sized up what we offered, 12 small certified-organic family farms pooling their produce to market direct to the customer, and she voiced her doubts. She was used to allowing only single farms to join her family of vendors. But she sized me up too and found something she liked or trusted, so she said, "Okay, but only as long as you bring all the farmers in to sell at your stand through the season." "Sure," I promised having gotten a foot in the door. It wasn't to be, of course; only one or two farmers bothered to come in at all, but the first season was a roaring success for the co-op as a fledgling sales organization. I made sure we stayed on Elizabeth's good side—as one had to— and, over several years, Elizabeth and I developed a wonderful mutual respect. I was awed by her tight control of the market, her fairness, her discipline with slack vendors, her amazing vision in holding it all together and bringing people together.

"Peter, I'd like you to meet Jamie Kennedy."

"Peter, can any of your farmers supply three bushels of romano beans for a dinner for seventy-five this Friday?"

She would often call up and tell me about the latest new vendors that she was excited to have visited. She had such respect for farmers and for food produced honestly and in a fresh way. And she would ask my opinion and advice. Early on at market, I incurred her wrath. She had strong rules and enforced them. Vendors were not allowed to sell before the bell rang, right at 3:00 p.m. As I tried to sneak in a sale for a customer who was running off to work, a booming voice bellowed out from the other side of the park: "Mr. Finch, the market opens at three o'clock, and not before!" Last year, held up in traffic and running late in setting up, I upheld her rule when an impending storm told her to ring the bell early. "No, Elizabeth, that's not fair; I'm not ready," I pleaded. She agreed to wait, and for weeks after, she deferred to me to see if I was ready before ringing the bell. A softening, maybe? I feel deep down that she truly respected her senior farmers, and I was lucky enough to have been in that number.

Elizabeth slipped away from us, succumbing to cancer, but her amazing energy, drive and spirit would remain with us as we tried to honour her legacy and continued to provide for the table she set for us so passionately. It had been an honour and a privilege to know her; hard to believe that she wouldn't be shuffling along on a glorious spring afternoon on opening day of market in May and that her voice wouldn't be greeting me across the park: "Peter, who do you have helping you today? I'd like to introduce you to …"

Elizabeth has left her mark. In her role as farmers-market

manager, that mark bluntly said yes to organics and no to genetically modified foods. It was now up to her successors at Evergreen Brick Works and Riverdale Farm to live up to her exacting standards by continuing to promote organic food and not allowing GM ingredients. Increasingly, it was becoming a case of either–or. Unless GMOs were mandated by government to be labelled and continued to be prohibited at market, organic certification would remain the only proof that foods at our farmers markets are GMO-free.

It is often the chefs and food writers that win the accolades and get the glory, perhaps rightly so, as food ingredients, presentation and innovation are so important and can be exhilarating. Largely underappreciated and unheralded are the many farmers that year after year do the spade work, planning their crop rotations, preparing the soil in the fields, planting the seeds, weeding the crops, growing the food and harvesting for market in the first place. Most of the organic growers I am privileged to know—my fellow farmers—are dedicated, passionate, perennially positive, extremely hard-working and humble. They get up with the sun, toil and trade through the hot days of summer, and fall into bed spent every night. Honest as the day is long, they are the salt of the earth, paragons of virtue in a cynical world. Included in their number are third-generation farmers Ben and Jessie Sosnicki, the van der Heyden family from Wooler Dale Farm, and the enterprising folks at Everdale. Paying a premium each year to submit a detailed application and be inspected to have their crops and products qualify as certified organic, they set the gold standard in healthy food production, and they tirelessly bring their bounty to market in all weathers.

Rainbow blessing the fields

An organic farm, properly speaking, is not one that uses certain methods and substances and avoids others; it is a farm whose structure is formed in imitation of the structure of a natural system that has the integrity, the independence and the benign dependence of an organism. (Wendell Berry, *The Gift of Good Land*)

It was gratifying to see the progress we had made in the dozen years that we had been tending our cherished patch of land. There had never ever been chemicals spread here. Carman, who owned and then rented the land for growing a variety of crops, always farmed traditionally even though surrounded by a sea of "conventional" farms. We had begun growing garlic and lavender, then echinacea, before settling on market-fresh greens and culinary and medicinal herbs as our mainstay and setting up shop as Rolling Hills Organics, certified organic all the way.

We were now selling twice weekly at organic farmers markets in the city (Toronto), an hour and a half away. We were selling to a handful of upscale city restaurants, and I was making weekly deliveries to several local eateries (in Warkworth, Cobourg and Port Hope on Rice Lake). I could genuinely promise all customers only fresh organic produce of premium quality, picked that day or the day previous, washed in pure well water, spun, dried, weighed, bagged, cooled and delivered.

Having retired the beast of a BCS walking tractor which did double duty as rototiller and sickle-bar mower, the grunt work on the farm was now ably performed by our labour-saving New Holland blue tractor (I wish it were red like my old Massey Ferguson) with its 72-inch tiller, cultivator, plow and bush hog, not to mention the front-end loader with its lugging capacity. Two hoop houses now supplied mostly salad greens and fresh herbs from mid-April to mid-December, extending our growing and selling season from six months to nine. A third hoop house would help us better keep up with demand. There was always next year. Elsewhere, five acres of fields retreed six years before with white and red pine, spruce and larch were really coming along, even if somewhat patchily. This year, beekeeper Ian Critchell placed 10 beehives next to the upper fields, so the bees were back (since previous owner Paul Von Baich's six hives and wonderful honey had moved away) and busy. The delicious, nutritious natural honey was moving well at market, where we hoped it would soon be joined by fresh-frozen bee pollen. Raw, unpasteurized and featuring nectar from wild flowers, alfalfa, lilac, apple, linden, goldenrod, aster, clover and buckwheat, amongst others, the honey was full of enzymes, vitamins and minerals.

Climb the mountains and get their good tidings. Nature's peace will flow into you as sunshine flows into trees. The wind will blow their own freshness into you, and the storms their energy, while cares will drop off like autumn leaves. (John Muir)

At the end of October, off we ventured once more on our annual pilgrimage to the best of Ontario's semiwilderness parks, this year for the first time to spectacular Killarney.

The afternoon paddle to our campsite home for the next four nights and days was leisurely as we glided over translucent aqua waters against a backdrop of vibrant October leaves and a deep blue sky. Arrived and settled in, we saw the late afternoon sun sliding down to the west and an orange glow illuminating the white quartzite mountains lined up on the north side of Killarney Lake. Dotted with a variety of trees in resplendent autumnal colours, the bumpy ridges increasingly electrified as purple shadings alternated with ever deeper sun-dappled ochres and burned golds.

Canoeists heading in late afternoon to their campsites on Killarney Lake

High Up in the Rolling Hills

We sat perched on our rock face overlooking the deep blue waters stretched out below, sipping a beer as dusk descended, and then, wow, the plumpest full moon popped up over the dark silhouette of white pines on the eastern horizon. The waters rippled in a frisson of vibration as a faint breeze whistled through the trees.

The campfire, primed with paper and twigs for kindling and rafts of scoured dry branches from the lakeside was ceremoniously lit. Sparks drifted up through the high pines and faded into the night air. Our senses blazed with the wonder of being truly out there, wrapped in the welcoming embrace of ancient rock, primal forest, clear lakes and open skies that revealed worlds, planets, constellations, nebulae beyond our tiny temporal home. For this fleeting moment in time, at this pure place, we were at centre stage, truly here and now, supremely alive and transfixed by the beauty of it all.

This trip marked the eighth successive year of autumn canoeing and camping for David and me, the paddle pals.

> For I have learned
> To look on nature, not as in the hour
> Of thoughtless youth; but hearing oftentimes
> The still, sad music of humanity,
> Nor harsh nor grating, though of ample power
> To chasten and subdue. And I have felt
> A presence that disturbs me with the joy
> Of elevated thoughts; a sense sublime
> Of something far more deeply interfused,
> Whose dwelling is the light of setting suns,
> And the round ocean and the living air,
> And the blue sky, and in the mind of man;
> A motion and a spirit, that impels

All thinking things, all objects of all thought,
And rolls through all things. Therefore am I still
A lover of the meadows and the woods,
And mountains; and of all that we behold
From this green earth; of all the mighty world
Of eye, and ear,-both what they half create,
And what perceive; well pleased to recognise
In nature and the language of the sense,
The anchor of my purest thoughts, the nurse,
The guide, the guardian of my heart, and soul
Of all my moral being.

(William Wordsworth, From "Lines Composed a Few Miles above Tintern Abbey," 1798)

11

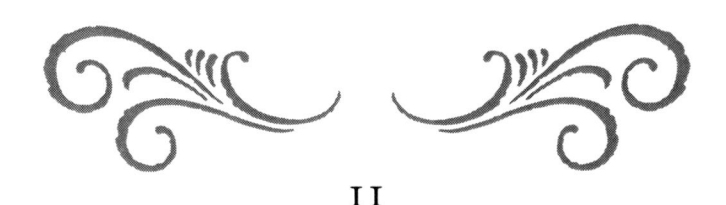

Looking Back, Moving Forward

Whenever we need to make a very important decision, it is best to trust to impulse, to passion, because reason usually tries to remove us from our dream, saying that the time is not yet right. Reason is afraid of defeat, but intuition enjoys life and its challenges. (Paulo Coelho)

By middle age, we have made a journey prompted by sober judgment and caution. But to feel most alive, we need to take risks so we keep from stagnating and so we continue to grow as individuals and maintain our childlike playfulness. To me, it is important to seek out challenges to prevent lethargy or conceit. Peaks and valleys lie ahead; let's not just move meekly forward. This is the motivating challenge that yields the reward of contentment.

Voyage through Life

Time was, when, blessed with rubber limbs and rechargeable hearts, we'd cavort, like crazy clockwork chimps, little legs running rampant in the sand, tiny bundles of nakedness carving our innocent scrawls and squiggles, throwaway fancies fed to the gobbling froth that surged and bubbled around our toes, sucking away our child's play into the slurpy endless sea, where, one day, time came to set sail as virgin seafarers released to the pitch and roll, hypnotic creaking of the mast; cast adrift, free-floating, we peered down into ink-blue depths, glazed profoundly into the sun's cauldron core, into the moon's wistful soul; in empty hours with no horizons we saw mysteries unfurl, yet still failed to recapture those carefree slippery fishes which darted deep in the bottomless below, so we set our course by the stars, fate tempered by will, and snaked along curving coasts, snuggled in the cozy bed of far-off coves, sipped of their bounty in dripping southern heat, returned to be awed by pure majesty in icy northern white, each day bringing new discovery and one more visionary voyage; we painted patterns charting our course, made maps of our world, embellished them with loving care, enchanted place names like Zihuatanejo, Bali, Yelapa, Ometepe, Villarrica, Dominical, Naxos, added colour-coded sense; as worms secrete silk we left a lifeline in our wake, each port of call a neat stitch pulled in by the anchor, dreams touching base, our creations framed by the bounds of beauty and time, taking us traversing great circles, climbing contours, winding in meanders within our delicate cocoons, threads ahead tugging us forward like a guiding light which completes circles, delivers us back home, where we store our maps of memory and longing, those burning montages which glow in the dark like embers with breath of gold and declare that time will come to take our place once more as timeless twinkles in the heavens, sparklers scribbling wisps of light, blazing down as memories of our cherished worldly home.

(This stream of consciousness originated somewhere in my mind in 1985.)

Now that I'm in my mid-fifties in the second decade of the 21st century, my body is telling me to ease up on the pace. In the thick of the growing season, my back aches from stooping, my neck is sore from tension, my arm pulses with overexertion, and then my shoulder throbs with pain from a muscle tear. My ticker pumps harder and my lungs puff away. My head is muddied by all the things on the to-do list today. I try to maintain my focus; no slip-ups, no blunders; there's no time for that. Names begin to elude me infuriatingly. How can that be? (It will come back to me … and it does, in the middle of the night as I lie wide awake churning over the busy morrow).

Yet as each new spring comes around, I'm raring to go again, up for the challenge. Planning, preparing the ground for the busy season ahead, sowing, planting. I crank up the tractor again and marvel at the seagulls following the turned-over soil. The weather guides me, and I tune in to the cycle of the seasons. I've got the rhythm now. Yes, I can handle this for a good few years yet.

As my dear old mum used to sing robustly as she worked her way through her housework:

Oh what a beautiful morning,
Oh what a beautiful day,
I've got a wonderful feeling,
Everything's going my way.

Plaque at the site of a 14th century longhouse

Just around the corner and up the hill from our farm is a plaque memorializing the site of a longhouse from the 14th century, long before Europeans came and laid their covetous hands on these parts and co-opted and renamed the site as the Richardson Site. The plaque's text reveals that this "was a palisaded village inhabited ca. AD 1300 by a few hundred Iroquoian farmers. From here, villagers travelled to Rice Lake to fish, fowl, hunt and socialize with people from nearby communities. They also collected berries, nuts, and other plant products to supplement their corn (maize) crops and to make medicines. During its occupancy, the village enlarged to cover 0.4 ha (1 acre), double its original size. Trent University archaeologists have uncovered traces of the village palisade, which encircled and protected the residential longhouses, as well as pottery, tools, food refuse, and other evidence for the daily living activities and beliefs of these early native farmers."

The village sounds idyllic, especially the communality, but it must have been a hard life. I am excited to think that here on this same land where our humble small farm grows food in the early 21st century, Native people were already farming and feeding themselves and their community some 700 years ago.

Climate and nature reshape the landscape over time. The human race does the same, but ever faster and more indiscriminately. Forests are turned to farmland, food and fuel production; open land to paved-over development. And now the sullying influence—especially degradation of the air, water and soil—of modern-day advanced technologies is also accelerating changes. In our radical and rapid reshaping, we have generally not given adequate priority to protection and conservation of nature for wholesome food, for our souls, for our fellow species and for our future.

A landmark report of the International Assessment of Agricultural Science and Technology for Development (IAASTD), commissioned by the United Nations and World Bank and involving more than 400 scientists and 30 governments, concludes definitively that small-scale farms and ecological farming methods provide the way forward to overcome the current food crisis and meet the needs of local communities. At last, a global assessment independent of corporate influence has acknowledged that farming has diverse natural, environmental and social functions.

Settlement of the land and changing patterns of usage are inevitable. However, well-planned development is sustainable and happens predominantly in and around main towns and commercial areas. We should be dotting the precious mixed-use rural landscape with more and more local food production units—small farms in harmony with nature. Shorelines, waterways, wetlands, forests, hills, valleys, open land should all be rigorously maintained and conserved. Only by using nature's tools—untreated seeds, pure soils, fresh air, fresh water—can we achieve this.

Author Frederick Philip Grove experienced Canada not as a wilderness but as a remote, wild, vibrantly beautiful homeland. To him it was a neighbourhood, albeit an odd one where caribou outnumbered people, where man, woman and nature long ago came to terms with one another to form relationships to the land that demanded the luxury of space. Within that vast territory of the spirit, in the solitude of the prairie, Grove discovered what it meant to be of this place.

To know a people, Lawrence Durrell once said, you need only a little patience, a quiet moment and a place where you might listen to the whispered messages of the land. Landscape, he thought, held the key to character. In the din of extraction and consumption, too many places and peoples with their ancient languages and traditions are falling silent in our own lifetimes.

Peak oil is the much-discussed point at which the maximum rate of global oil extraction is reached and after which the rate of production enters terminal decline. Even if peak oil is not immediately upon us, the peak of oil below $100 per barrel almost certainly is. Smart conservation of fossil fuels and a slowing down of the juggernaut of economic growth make sound sense in planning and facilitating a more sustainable future for generations to come. Under the pretext of defending against terrorism, predatory hawks continue to manoeuver for control of the black gold, gas and other resources in Iraq, strategic Afghanistan, Libya, Syria, Iran and wide-open Africa, stirring up scorn and plundering as they go. New oil and gas fields to fight over come into play in Eurasia, in the eastern Mediterranean, in the South China Sea and elsewhere. And, closer to home, hydraulic fracturing, or fracking, for shale oil and methane gas is now ripping up huge swaths of land, bringing jobs in the short term but a new barrage of calamitous environmental consequences for the long term.

The federal government of Canada and the provincial government of Alberta have been sanctioning to industry and promoting to the world what they mischievously label "ethical" oil—so called merely because it does not originate from the Middle East—scraped out at huge environmental and economic cost from thousands of square kilometres of Alberta tar sands that were until recently covered in virgin forest. This vast area continues to be cleared, drained and strip-mined for tar sands close to the surface. Ever more land over vast tracts is being fragmented into a spiderweb of seismic lines, roads, pipelines and well pads from in situ drilling projects.

The tar sands, a mixture of crude bitumen (a semisolid form of crude oil), silica sand, clay minerals and water, are turned into crude oil in an extremely energy-intensive way and producing enormous greenhouse gas emissions. They are located beneath boreal forest, a complex ecosystem that comprises a unique mosaic of forest, wetlands and lakes. Canada's ribbon of boreal forest is globally significant, and until tar-sands projects ripped it asunder, represented one-quarter of the world's remaining intact forests. At present rates of drawing, the water sucked from the natural environment to drive this dirty oil industry will be gone in a few short years, and it is already dangerously depleted. The sun may well set on the tar sands sooner rather than later.

Beyond the ecosystem services the world's third largest watershed provides in this vast Athabasca region (cleansing water, producing oxygen and storing carbon), it is home to a wide variety of wildlife, including bears, wolves, lynx and some of the largest populations of woodland caribou left in the world. Its wetlands and lakes provide a habitat for 30 percent of North America's songbirds and 40 percent of its waterfowl. The development of the tar sands sacrifices the natural wild landscape, and along with it the wild animals, fish, Lake Athabasca and the entire Athabasca River basin. As a direct result of the highly toxic effluent that runs off into the ground and the poisons emitted into the air, sacrificed also is the health of Native peoples, particularly the Cree, Dene and Metis, who have lived here, hunting and fishing, for centuries, as large numbers of those living downstream in communities like Fort Chipewyan and Fort MacKay develop hitherto rare strains of cancer and other autoimmune diseases.

Andrew Nikiforuk writes in *Tar Sands*, "Bitumen development will never be sustainable. The megaproject will eventually destroy or industrialize a forest the size of Florida and diminish the biological diversity and hydrology of the region forever … A business-as-usual case for the tar sands will change Canada forever. It will enrich a few powerful companies, hollow out the economy, destroy the world's third-largest watershed, industrialize nearly one-quarter of Alberta's landscape, consume the last of the nation's natural gas supplies, and erode Canadian sovereignty."

I ponder whether I have reached the maximum rate of return after which returns enter a terminal decline—peak life? Have living standards for many of us reached peak abundance? Is the big bubble about to burst? My generation has certainly borrowed much from the future and from the planet. The debts to be repaid are astronomical, and it is certain that they cannot be fully retired, at least at current punitive interest rates and current accelerated rates of destruction. Governments and mega-corporations—now in the developing world as well as the developed—plough through finite natural resources like there is no tomorrow.

Intensified industrial technologies have been aggravating

unintended consequences for the ecosystem: air pollution, nuclear waste, radiation contamination, extreme weather events, desertification, acidification of the oceans, ravaging of fossil-fuel reserves, poisoning and depletion of soils and farmland, loss of flora and fauna habitat (and biodiversity). With these upheavals and losses go peak food, peak soils, peak health. It is simply not feasible for us to maintain our general well-being by turning our backs on the natural world. The truly wondrous biodiversity and plenty that recent generations inherited have been savaged by feverish greed in the quest for short-term gain. Long gone are those vast herds of bison roaming the wide-open North American grasslands, great auks patrolling the seas and passenger pigeons swarming in the skies. Wild salmon, cod, whales, sharks and turtles are disappearing from the oceans. Domesticated and farmed surrogates of wild creatures are no real substitute. With the animals and plants goes the heritage of ancient cultures, languages and whole ways of life that had been passed down over millennia. Which species is next to be rendered extinct by this orgy of wastefulness? The caribou? The hippopotamus? The rhinoceros? The elephant? The panda? The gorilla? The tiger? The polar bear? The penguin? The whale? The tuna? The butterflies? The bees? The frogs? All of the above?

Humans have been killing other animals and slaughtering our own kind for as long as we have stood upright. But only in the last half century or so have we developed the capacity to extinguish not merely a species or a tribe, but whole floras and faunas. With the burning of fossil fuels, the splitting of atoms, the synthesizing of chemicals unknown in nature, the genetic engineering of organisms, and the headlong growth of our own population, we are disrupting all the life-sustaining processes on Earth. As our actions throw into disarray the conditions that have nurtured humankind for hundreds of thousands of years, what conditions will replace them? (Scott Russell Sanders, *Buffalo Eddy*)

What are we learning from the tsunamis, the earthquakes, the volcanoes, the floods, the droughts, the tornadoes, the typhoons, the hurricanes? We should react to these extreme workings of nature with some humility and a determination to rebuild and adapt. When we witness melting glaciers, ice sheets and polar caps; massive oil spills; radiation leaks from damaged nuclear plants; and extreme weather volatility across the planet, we would be wise to take a hard look at our world, size up the gravity of the situation and set out systems to mitigate the severity of the threats. As we witness the poisoning of our bodies and the poisoning of our planet's lands and oceans, it only makes sense to make substantive changes to the way we live our lives. Our governments, drowning in debt and consistently sucked in by unrestrained multinational corporations, are driving us not away from but into the storm dragging us in a downward spiral. In tandem, governments and corporations lead us toward the brink, just as the herders led the buffaloes to the cliff to jump to their fate.

As Bob Dylan famously wrote and sang some fifty years ago now:

> I heard the sound of a thunder, it roared out a warnin'
> I heard the roar of a wave that could drown the whole world
> ...
> And it's a hard rain's a-gonna fall.

It is possible to get off the slippery slope we are on, and a raft of responsible groups, writers, activists, filmmakers and communities are indeed taking a noble stand. Prolonged decline is eminently preventable with a return to healthy policy, sound planning, just governance, adequate foresight and sensible regulation from the top down. Given a common will, using the precautionary principle as primary guide, we can avert approaching threats. Above all, we must commit to conserving the natural world that remains. It really does matter how we protect—or conversely, how we despoil—Greenland's and Antarctica's massive ice sheets, Brazil's and Indonesia's rainforests, and, yes, the Athabascan Basin's boreal forests. They are all interconnected and influence the web that is life on earth. Likewise, how we protect or despoil soils, farmland, water sources and the oceans and how we save seeds, grow food and harvest crops on farms large and small all truly matter in sustaining good health.

Albert Einstein noted that "the definition of stupidity is doing the same thing over and over again and expecting different results." Is this the age of peak waste, peak stupidity, peak greed? Let's hope so.

We have to adapt as a society to do what is required to sustain life on earth: to tend the soil and oceans, conserve our dwindling natural resources and what is left of our flora and fauna, feed ourselves and harness renewable wind and sun and water and geothermal energy. Our ability to do so is in doubt given our history but eminently possible if true commitment and cooperation can counter short-term greed. We have the technology to make use of renewable sources of energy, but they are being blocked from development and uptake by petty politics. Humankind has decided negatively on the fate of other species; this is a choice that will determine the fate of our own. Enough of the green-washers with their endless hollow slogans and platitudes! Their toxic coat of paint simply glosses over deep-rooted issues.

Skeptics and naysayers spin their spin and government stalls innovation, all the time imposing ever more onerous restrictions on local and personal governance. Simultaneously, far-sighted communities, both rural and urban, in other parts of the world have taken vast strides toward energy independence and nature preservation. They have embraced a fresh start; they have brought people together, mobilized them and made the move away from fossil-fuel dependence to alternative means of transportation and totally renewable energy; away from chemical farming to natural, organic farming; away from overconsumption and mindless wastefulness and toward a well-planned, viable future.

> *We do not have to visit a madhouse to find disordered minds; our planet is the mental institution of the universe.* (Johann Wolfgang von Goethe)

As Voltaire's *Candide* made clear: *"Il faut cultiver notre jardin."* Yes, we must look after our garden. To me, this means starting on our own plot. Hope lies in gathering ever more gardeners to plant seeds and trees and in conserving and regenerating all natural resources, especially the sacred forests and oceans. Hope lies in using the sun, wind, rain, waters and geothermal energy. Such cultivation represents our best chance of generating a healthy future for the next generations that includes nature.

We need to send out SOSs. Soils built up over millennia are being destroyed by chemicals and subsumed under concrete as suburban developments reach out into the countryside and swallow up swaths of prime farmland. *Save our soils.* And just five mega-corporations now control 75 percent of the world's seed supply. When they eventually own the remaining 25 percent (those that are wild, unclaimed, public, owned by smallholders), that is the end of any freedom farmers and individuals have in the food they grow and where they buy it. *Save our seeds.* There are many visionaries calling these out, but Vandana Shiva is surely the champion. *The future of our world depends on how we steward our land, soil, water, and seeds, and pass them on to future generations.* (Dr. Vandana Shiva)

Imagine a world in which individuals, landowners, gardeners and farmers were prohibited from growing and selling garlic, fresh herbs, herbal teas, honeys, fermented foods, pickles, oils and vinegars and natural creams, salves and ointments because naturally grown plants and plant products were patented and the rights to them owned and licensed by corporations or governments. Imagine a world in which nature were privately owned. Well, that world is increasingly upon us now—with the overzealous regulation and restriction of natural products, the patenting of crops, the corporate ownership of seeds and food, the escalating genetic modification of foods, the killing of the bees. It really is the end of nature as we have known it.

We have already consumed 90 percent of the big fish in the ocean. Today's industrial-scale net catches are rapaciously sucking up the remaining 10 percent. This is, of course, calamitous. The legendary Jacques Cousteau has passed on, but hopefully Cousteau family members like Jacques' son Jean-Michel and grandson Philippe can carry the torch for ocean conservation and remain visible, passionate champions the part of the world that blesses us with life-giving minerals and foods.

Hubris led us to believe that the abundance of nature was infinite. Human greed and folly wiped out millions upon millions of mammals, birds and amphibians, eradicating thousands of species and taking many others to the brink of extinction. Now we have turned on the billions of honeybees that provide so much of our food through the simple act of pollinating fruits, berries, nuts and vegetables. As humans, we have a symbiotic relationship with bees (through foods from plants), so it is critical that we protect them.

In the pursuit of higher yields, industrial agriculture is now so dependent on the pollinating powers of honeybees that continued precipitous decline in bee populations could jeopardize our food supply. It is hard to imagine a world in which the coffee, tea and orange juice we enjoy with our morning breakfast are scarce, and we cannot begin to envisage the impact of much-reduced production of apples, citrus fruits, grapes, peaches, cherries, melons, nuts, squash, beans, carrots, sunflowers and, yes, honey.

Big Agriculture has used the industry of bees to perform on a colossal scale, producing astounding harvests of all these crops. In the United States, fruit farmers pay commercial beekeepers to truck bees thousands of miles to pollinate their crops. Early every year, millions of bees are trucked from the East Coast to the West Coast to pollinate the vast plantations of almond trees heavily laced with pesticides and then back for a detox in Georgia before being trucked off again to the Northeast to pollinate the apple crop. No wonder bees' systems are overloaded! Commercial beekeepers are reporting continued sharp declines in bee populations year after year. Some have replenished with stocks from Australia. In China, in the province of Sichuan, pear trees have been pollinated by hand since the overuse of pesticides in the 1980s wiped out the honeybee population. Is this what we are heading toward in North America?

If a rich variety of popular foods and flowers do not get pollinated, our diets will consist of lots of rice, wheat, corn and soy, which, coincidentally, are the main crops that the chemical giants have huge financial stakes in. Could the masters of the food system be out to control pollination as well as seeds and crops?

It can be no coincidence that the commercial beekeepers who isolated their hives from the chemical spraying of crops have reported only minimal bee losses. Similarly, the hives of organic and biodynamic beekeepers who work on diversified systems of food production and strive to enhance the immune systems of their bees have also not suffered significant losses. Honeybees have lived successfully on the planet for millions of years until this point in time. Bees are the ultimate selfless workers, and they provide the miracle of honey. The implications of its contribution to medicine are still emerging. As individuals and farmers, we can help the honeybee. Apart from working to ban indiscriminate spraying of pesticides and the planting of GM crops and to promote organic agriculture, planting native flowers, trees and shrubs that are bee-friendly in our gardens and fields is important. We can learn about beekeeping and get hives going in our own backyards. We can grow, buy and eat food that supports local, organic and small-scale agricultural practices and producers. When we take care of the honeybee, we take care of ourselves.

2011

Naxos in the Cyclades

It was refreshing to get away for a few weeks in the winter to two Greek islands. Despite the islanders' being enmeshed in Greece's debt crisis, these are still beautiful tucked-away places where life goes on largely traditionally, seasonally and locally, beyond the din. Although we had spent an acclimatizing week on verdant Paros, nothing prepared us for the bold drama of the neighbouring island of Naxos. From the moment the ship rounded the northern tip of Paros at Naoussa and the jagged peaks around Naxos town loomed on the horizon, we were held in her thrall. The island threw up a mixed bag of weather in this pre-spring off-season. The Aegean sun illuminated the brilliant whitewashed and electric-blue houses, the verdant landscape and the omnipresent white marble. Cool northerly gusts whipped up the dark blue sea, and then grey scudding clouds swooped down over the high peaks and torrential showers passed over and by.

We delighted in slipping into the slow pace as we rambled along narrow winding streets, rustic roads, country paths and lonely beaches free of summer hordes.

In a rented Fiat Panda, we set out to visit Koronos, perched in the mountains, and Lionas, a pretty cove, a drive of some 9 kilometres below. Our route through the high towns of Chalki, Filoti and Apiranthos took us along asphalted, seriously twisting roads with breathtaking vistas, often way down to the glistening blue ocean below. The mountainsides were strewn with rocks and boulders and criss-crossed by stone walls demarcating property, even high on precipices.

In Koronos, hostess Matine cooked delectable dishes from her own greens, potatoes, cheese, village lamb and pork. Her taverna was abuzz with loud oratory, thick with smoke. She put us up in the simple suite of a renovated house in the village. Down on the beach in Lionas, Gundi was entranced by the most interesting beach for rock-picking she had ever combed. The weathered, marbled pebbles varied in their tones of earth and white; they gleamed in their coats of seawater. I wandered off to just perch and ponder in the marble amphitheatre above the vibrant green sea. What a joy to be here at the wild edge of a Greek island, where a sturdy land steeped in history and myth met a swirling, fabled sea. At night, the glow of the village illuminated the massive rock face to the south of the cove as darkness enveloped the sea, and the whooshing of the waters below, the whistling of the wind above continued unabated.

Lionas on Naxos in the Cyclades, Greece

One lively evening in Lionas, at the Delfinaki taverna of Manolis and Vasso Koufopoulos, English-speaking resident Apostoulos taught us of the concepts of *filoxenia* and *aftarkis*. He said these are both especially well-honed on Naxos. Manolis's fine fresh rosé wine flowed freely, and Apostoulos acted as interpreter not only of language but also of cultural refinements. He explained that *filoxenia*, which literally means "love of strangers," is what Naxians, and Greeks, welcome visitors with. Once they warm to you, their hearts and souls open up and wrap you in a blanket of stoic insight. Filoxenia is a generosity of spirit, a joyful, sharing attitude that Greeks take great pride in as a defining attribute. Manolis spent over 30 years mining emery from within the local mountains. Now he was a proud farmer and food producer. He beamed as he brought us olives from the family trees, rosé wine made from the family grapes, honey produced by the family bees, eggs from the family chickens, meat and cheese from his brother's goats and sheep. And filoxenia was a main reason that he loved to provide this bounty and that Vasso loved to cook it.

Aftarkis is an ancient word that literally means "sufficient in oneself." It describes a person who, through discipline, has discovered resources within to cope with any eventuality. Naxians display this quality probably because of the challenges of surviving and sustaining a livelihood, community and culture on a mountainous island.

Naxos is blessed to be the most fertile island of the Cyclades. It has a good supply of water in a region where water is usually inadequate. Mount Zas, at 999 metres, is the highest peak in the Cyclades, and it tends to trap the clouds, generating greater rainfall. This has made agriculture important to the economy, with growing various vegetable and fruit crops as well as breeding cattle and rearing sheep and goats making Naxos the most self-sufficient island of the group. Grapes, oranges, lemons, limes, figs and olives find ideal conditions and locals not only eat the fruit but also make precious wine and olive oil from it. Tomatoes, potatoes, peppers and cucumbers all grow robustly here. Growing wild on the hillsides throughout the island are sage, rosemary, thyme, oregano and giant fennel. Yellow-flowering clover carpets the soil between the olive and citrus trees. Beekeepers produce a delectable thyme honey, especially renowned in Gundi's favourite little mountain village of Keramoti, so picturesquely located in its high verdant valley. Farmers make milk, cheese, butter and yogurt and provide succulent chicken, pork, lamb and beef. Fishermen bring in an array of fish large and small and squid, octopus and shrimp, although catches were much smaller by the time we visited than they had been. This all makes for a local food culture which is vibrant, hearty and sustained by each succeeding generation of wonderful cooks. Portions are generally overly generous. Naxians love their food and wine, and they love to share it. Filoxenia was alive and well on Naxos for our visit.

The Greek islands captivated us and call us to come back one day. We returned from our sojourn heartened and refreshed but barely warmed by the mixed bag of pre-spring weather. We were ill-prepared for the nasty cold, wet spring and for the sudden hot dryness of early summer that followed on its heels. Despite good preparation with the help of the briefly returning Toby, the plants said, "No way; too cool." Early plantings quickly gave up the ghost. Early production from the hoop houses went to waste as it all came at once before markets were up and running. However, we stuck at it, as one has to in this game of ebb and flow played by unpredictable weathers and temperamental plants. And we were rewarded, as always, by understanding, loyal and appreciative customers at market and by willing help on the farm, this year from locals Jerrica, Leigh and Lukash.

The first full season of Riverdale farmers market after the passing of dear Elizabeth Harris was a slow one. Although we had cooperative weather on market days, her presence was sorely missed. We concentrated our efforts on meeting growing demand from the Saturday Brick Works market, where traffic just kept on increasing. We're a small farm and want to stay that way, so we were not willing or able to ramp up production much more. If I were a younger farmer, I would be investing heavily, hiring extra staff, boosting production and expanding markets. But we were happy where we were at the time—running a sustainable business and enjoying a simple and satisfying lifestyle, relishing our seasons growing greens and herbs, and setting down roots in the Northumberland Hills. With Marina Queirolo as food program manager, the overseeing Evergreen Foundation moved the Don Valley Brick Works Farmers Market forward. Through Elizabeth, Brick Works started out purely as an organic market, but its management was doing a stellar job of educating the next generation of city dwellers about nature in their midst, attracting ever more customers to the farmers market, and operating myriad other programs and events. As a committed organic farmer, I pressed the indispensable value of certified organic not only as a way to farm in a truly ecological way but also as our best way to ensure safe, full-flavoured food loaded with nutrients and devoid of chemical and synthetic additives and genetically modified ingredients and as the best way to preserve our health, that of our customers, and that of our communities and the planet at large.

Farmers markets are, of course, characteristic of the wider picture of all whole-foods markets, where "natural" is promoted as the panacea in the grey areas left by the lack of mandatory labelling of genetically modified products. The consumer's only recourse in avoiding GMOs is, as I've noted elsewhere, to buy and eat products that are certified organic, GMOs being banned by legislation from all produce labelled as organic. Thanks to Big Industry's colossal funding of a massive, deceptive propaganda campaign against mandatory GMO labelling of foods in California, Californians were to vote in late 2012 to reject Proposition 37. They thereby acquiesced to continued blindfolding in their food purchase decisions. So be it. Proponents of these labels viewed them as a potential route to force GM-food producers to come clean on a broader scale. However, further independent study and further consumer-led pressure on the issue will ultimately turn the tide in favour of clear labelling of all foods. In the meantime, buy organic.

As the Organic Consumers Association notes in "Whole Foods and the Myth of *Natural*" at http://www.organicconsumers.org/whole_foods_unfi.cfm:

The $25 billion organic marketplace has enjoyed substantial growth for over a decade, thanks to growing consumer consciousness and farmer innovation. No longer a passing trend or simply a niche market, organic food and farming are proving to be a viable alternative to the unhealthy, unsustainable and unjust conventional food system ... Consumers are confused about the difference between conventional products marketed as "natural" and those nutritionally and environmentally superior products that are "certified organic" ... A troubling trend in organics today is the calculated shift on the part of certain large companies from certified organic ingredients and products to so-called "natural" products ... In the majority of cases, "natural" products are green-washed conventional products, with "natural" label claims neither policed nor monitored.

... Organic consumers are increasingly left without certified organic choices while organic farmers continue to lose market share to "natural" imposters.

...

Organic farmers must "get big or get out" to be able to compete and have free access to markets. Many industrial organic farms and dairy operations reflect the same abuses and problems of the conventional food system: extremely energy intensive, systematic abuse of workers, reduced food quality, and damage to biodiversity.

So-called "natural" products, since they are actually in most cases conventional products in disguise, are being sold at lower prices than genuine organic products—

thereby retarding the growth of the organic sector ... In light of the food system's significant contribution to the climate crisis and the deepening economic troubles facing local food economies, it is more important than ever to prioritize locally produced organic food.

People are taking a stand and saying no to GMOs. Just six countries—the United States of America, Argentina, Brazil, Canada, China and India—grow 99 percent of the world's genetically modified (GMO, or transgenic) crops. Canada, the country I call home, holds 7 percent of the total global acreage.

In 2009, The American Academy of Environmental Medicine (AAEM) released its position paper on genetically modified foods stating that "GM foods pose a serious health risk" and calling for a moratorium on GM foods. Citing several animal studies, the AAEM concludes that "there is more than a casual association between GM foods and adverse health effects" and that "GM foods pose a serious health risk in the areas of toxicology, allergy and immune function, reproductive health, and metabolic, physiologic and genetic health." Not a single clinical trial of GMOs on humans has been published.

The risks of GMO crops to humans and to the ecosystem are far from adequately documented, with almost all the studies a long way from independent, being fabricated by GMO manufacturers themselves and their apologists. However, there is a growing body of evidence that they are harmful and potentially fatal to certain birds, insects, fish and other wildlife. Transgenic *Bacillus thuringiensis* (Bt) pollen and glyphosate pesticide may be a root cause of epidemics such as bee colony collapse disorder, although manufacturers of GMOs and their proponents continue to deny this. Bee colonies have been dying off at the alarming rate of 30 to 40 percent a year in countries where GMO crops are widespread, such as the United States and Canada. If this unprecedented die-off continues, there will be no honeybees to pollinate crops which depend on them, particularly fruits, nuts and berries but also many vegetables. This is disastrous for our food supply. Fruits and vegetables are probably the most vital elements in our daily diet. Already their cost is prohibitive to many poor people around the world, who are malnourished as a result. Such malnutrition coincides with the recent obesity and diabetes epidemics brought on in part by the excessive amounts of sugars and starches in the diet from corn and soybeans, foods that are often genetically modified, bringing the scale of the scourge home.

Gundi and I have sworn off knowingly purchasing products containing added fructose or corn syrup because it is now probable that these foodstuffs are derived from GM corn. This means foregoing most processed foods in the supermarket, including a whole host of brand-name cereal products, snacks, canned and dried soups, potato chips and even some green-washed granola bars. As we amble, stunned, through the supermarket aisles, it is hard to find many foods that nourish or appeal. The fruits and vegetables we eat are organic whenever possible. The fact that GMO foods do not yet have to be labelled as such in our part of the world means that we have to be that much more vigilant in avoiding most packaged foods containing corn, soybeans and even modern dwarf strains of wheat. We now have to beware that fruits and vegetables sprayed by pesticides, fungicides, insecticides and herbicides now also hide genetic modification.

Some people claim that they're too busy to worry themselves about where their food comes from and what it is made of, don't believe it makes a difference, or just don't want to think about it. However, daily nutrition is key to overall health and well-being, far more so than the conventional medical establishment will acknowledge. For this reason, it is important to question the huge amounts of pharmaceutical and psychotropic drugs and chemical cocktails prescribed by the medical profession to deal with illness and disease, for these likewise affect long-term health.

Two examples of particularly dangerous GMO-containing foods are alfalfa and salmon. GMO alfalfa has already been approved in the United States and may be soon in Canada. GMO salmon is awaiting final approval in the United States but requires additional approval from Canada to proceed. Salmon are scheduled to be "manufactured" in laboratories on Prince Edward Island and grown to monster size in faraway Panama. (You've got to laugh at the absurdity of it all; genetically modified eggs grown in a lab in eastern Canada are shipped to Panama to grow into mock-up fish, shipped back to the United States and Canada for packaging and distribution across the continent, and perhaps around the world, to end up somewhere on your plate, disguised as real food.)

Genetically engineered (GE) salmon, which have been dubbed "Frankenfish," have been proposed for approval by the Food and Drug Administration. AquaBounty Technologies, headquartered in Massachusetts, is a biotechnology company that proposes to produce a hybrid Atlantic salmon modified with a growth gene from Chinook salmon and an antifreeze gene from ocean pout. The final approval of GE salmon could well represent a serious threat to the survival of native salmon populations, many of which have already suffered severe declines related to salmon farms and other human impacts. Wild Atlantic salmon are already on the endangered-species list in the United States; approval of these GE Atlantic salmon could be the final blow to wild stocks as modified genes meet wild ones, which will happen at some point. Additionally, the impacts to human health of eating GE fish are entirely unknown. When GE salmon are approved and unlabelled as such (the FDA has argued that these GE salmon don't even need to be labelled!) consumers are not in the position to make an informed food choice

The USDA has allowed the planting of genetically modified alfalfa, a crop used mainly as hay for cattle. The agency has claimed that Monsanto's weed-resistant Roundup Ready alfalfa is safe. The introduction of this Frankenfeed, even in the remote possibility that it were safe, puts the organic meat and dairy industries in severe jeopardy.

Alfalfa is a robust hay crop, loaded with minerals and all-round nutrition. Why modify it? Transgenic contamination of organic alfalfa could have economic consequences for the fast-growing, $20 billion a year organic milk industry because those dairies would lose their source of organic feed. Alfalfa pollen is notorious for dispersing freely, which means that GM alfalfa can easily spread to non-GM fields without permission from farm owners. And therein lies the issue. GM crops are incompatible with organic products. So, if GM alfalfa inadvertently ends up feeding cows bred to produce organic milk or beef, the organic nature of the product becomes sullied. Organic and sustainable farming advocates are challenging the decision by the USDA to fully deregulate Roundup Ready alfalfa, which is engineered to withstand the herbicide glyphosate. They fear that pollen drift and bees could cross-pollinate the altered alfalfa and natural varieties.

"Approving the unrestricted planting of GMO alfalfa is a blatant case of the USDA serving one form of agriculture at the expense of all others", said Ed Maltby, executive director of the Northeast Alliance of Organic Dairy Producers in a news release. "If this decision is not remedied, the result will be lost livelihoods for organic dairy farmers, loss of choice for farmers and consumers, and no transparency about GM contamination of our foods."

***

The world over, settlers that succeeded hunter-gatherers always farmed organically, even before the term was coined, to supply their communities with food right up until the aftermath of World War II, when chemical farming came into practice. In the 1950s onward, as the Anthropocene Era is said to have taken hold (around the time my own journey through life began), farmers in the developed world were coaxed by governments and new taskmasters in the form of large corporations into buying their leftover chemicals, as well as newly developed chemicals, to spread on the land. Farmers were desperate to start over after the war, and many signed on to the new model of industrial agriculture. Modern wheat has come a long way since the early varieties of spelt, kamut, emmer and einkorn. Dwarf strains of wheat developed in the United States and Mexico and now monopolizing North American wheat production were introduced in the 1950s and are the product of chemical mutagenesis. These genetic changes could be contributing to the rise in celiac disease, gluten sensitivity and the obesity epidemic we are seeing today.

With the promise of increased yields and the mirage of feeding the world, a Green Revolution was sold to farmers. Industrial agriculture took a firm grip and transformed the food system into a mass-market juggernaut. In the early 1970s, the US government, through Secretary of Agriculture Earl Butz, bullied farmers with the call to "get big or get out" and to plant "hedgerow to hedgerow." Now, some 40 years later, many of the claims of the misnomered Green Revolution ring hollow and have brought untold distress to countless farmers around the world and depletion of soils everywhere. Green Revolution agriculture relied on extensive use of pesticides to counter pest damage that inevitably occurred in mono-cropping. Its spread radically reduced both agricultural biodiversity and wild biodiversity. Wikipedia reveals that long-term exposure to pesticides such as organo-chlorines, creosote and sulfate have been correlated with higher cancer rates. Epidemiological studies in humans have linked phenoxy acid herbicides or contaminants in them with soft tissue sarcoma and malignant lymphoma; organo-chlorine insecticides with soft tissue sarcoma, non-Hodgkin's lymphoma, leukemia and, less consistently, with cancers of the lung and breast; organo-phosphorous compounds with non-Hodgkin's lymphoma and leukemia; and triazine herbicides with ovarian cancer.

And so, faced with this onslaught of potential health consequences from industrial agriculture (which the powers that be now have the gall to call "conventional farming"!), organic farmers are part of a growing band of determined folk who have adopted the traditional, common-sense, natural, small-scale, holistic ways of working the soil, looking after the land and growing food. A rapid spread of organic farming to take back the land is vital if we are to save our living soils from exhaustion and extinction. Mother Nature built up these soils for millennia, and we now need to sustain and replenish those that remain by growing nourishing food in them and caring for them.

Here at home, with help from locals, Gundi and I look after our small acreage in the hills and embrace this romantic vision. Both of us are fighting fit thanks to our natural, varied and balanced diet free of medication. We try to accentuate the positive and sprinkle our days with gratitude and wonder. I work with the land sowing seeds, planting plenty, and bring our healthy harvests to market, whilst Gundi continues to be captivated in her creation of beautiful works of glass art.

Eons ago, receding ice sheets left a glacial till in these hills that is mineral-rich and ideal for growing food. It is up to farmers everywhere to forego treating their land with chemicals and to continually work it up naturally into fertile, nutrient-dense living soil. We organic farmers do this by incorporating crop residues and other plant material like green manures, hay and straw mulch, and compost. Livestock farmers add animal manure. Nurturing a biodiverse environment replete with birds, bees and butterflies, we move our crops around, rotating them between fields to minimize damage from insects and to maximize fertility. Plants respond readily with robust growth. The recipe is really quite simple:

Ingredients: seeds, soil, sunshine, rain, fresh air.

Directions: Plant untreated seeds into soil that is alive with nutrients. Add sunshine, rain and fresh air.

Tend lovingly, allow space to grow and harvest when ripe.

Eat fresh, sell and share. Preserve surpluses.

Repeat annually or more frequently if desired.

High Up in the Rolling Hills

Killarney Lake, Killarney Provincial Park

We do it every year in the fall, this season of transformation: dive into the chilly air of the great outdoors of lakes and rocks, woodlands and wetlands, just as they are all bedding down for winter. It's a few days and nights of time out from routine and regularity, a breathing space. Our spouses think we have lost our senses; far from it, we know they are out there to be retrieved. The sense of connection runs deep. There is a kinship with the trees; the waters; the canoe that guides us; the ravens, beavers, ducks and loons that greet us; the 2-billion-year-old white quartzite rocks that cradle us; and the star-filled sky that parades at night.

The predations so prevalent in the troubled realm of humanity are purged from our thoughts for these few precious days. We are far removed from them out here in the pure wild. The true natives of these lands knew all too well that a profound respect for nature is key to survival.

Far-sighted visionaries in the last century set aside the almost

50,000 hectares of Killarney Provincial Park for many generations to behold in their pristine state, to share with the black bears and the beavers, the lynxes and the loons, the ravens and the rattlesnakes. This perfect fusion of earthly terrain and watery expanses has evolved without humanity over millions of years. Let's hope present-day and future generations allow it to continue sustain all manner of life for millennia to come.

> Two spirited ravens
> flap their timeworn wings
> and rise into the still clear air
> above glistening lakes,
> sun-dappled trees,
> rounded white quartzite ranges,
> two pilots on an endless flight,
> bound they know not where.

2012

After a delicious winter hiatus on the southwest coast of tropical Costa Rica (three weeks back to nature and *pura vida*), we returned home to decidedly unwintery conditions in February. For the first time, the ground never truly froze in the hoop houses. With buoyant market demand and Christina Temple all set to ramp up her business selling fresh local organic produce to her demanding network of Toronto chefs, it seemed a good year to expand production. Sales projections looked promising, and so we hired four seasonal helpers and ordered seeds aplenty.

Springtime was glorious. Big sister Jill came to visit from her home in Berlin for two weeks in May. She and I share core values, and it was a joy to see her immerse herself in the land and our place in it. We celebrated her presence and Gundi's and my birthdays with 20 friends and Greek food, music and dance.

Then, in June, with most of the early-season seeds planted and crops poking up, the rains abandoned us. The heat came, but the rains stayed away or passed us by. I watered, the plants stayed small and got grown in with weeds, and the workers fiddled away trying to remove them. And I watered, and the rains stayed away. It got hot, and I took to watering the greens every other day to keep them alive. They hung in there and provided a harvest. I gave up on rows and rows of colourful carrots and beets, chard and kale. And I watered … All June and July, there was barely a drop of rain. I sacrificed Riverdale farmers market, hearing that it was very slow anyway. By early August, things were getting bad. My continued promises to Chris and to customers at both farmers markets that we'd turn the corner did not help. Neither hoped-for rains nor any increase in volume of produce from the fields materialized. We let two of the four workers go. We stuck at it, rewarded by a good crop of fresh garlic, too many garlic scapes to sell and then plenty of dried garlic. Lavender obliged with a healthy harvest also. Everything else limped along or succumbed to the extended heat and lack of moisture. What a tough slog this growing season turned into!

Across the Midwest farm belt of the United States and up through eastern Canada and the Eastern Seaboard, it was full-on drought. Swaths of corn and soybeans roasted in the heat, browned and shrivelled. Some of the mega-farmers got away with it, and some were just a rainfall away from disaster, but overall, yields were pitiful. Some of the corn and soy boys were doing okay, but at what cost to the overall food supply? Wherever their crops matured fully, big paydays awaited them as global commodities markets sucked up their harvests to feed industrial feedlot cattle, automobiles with massively subsidized corn ethanol, and the voracious appetite of processors of high-fructose corn syrup for their packaged products. Only 2 percent of the GM soy in the

United States ends up feeding humans; the rest, like the corn, goes to feed factory-farmed animals and to run cars and trucks in the form of biodiesel fuel. The results of a 2011 National Academies of Sciences (NAS) study, entitled "Renewable Fuel Standard: Potential Economic and Environmental Effects of U.S. Biofuel Policy" show that neither ethanol nor biodiesel can replace much petroleum without having an impact on food supply. If all American corn and soybean production were dedicated to biofuels, that fuel would replace only 12 percent of gasoline demand and 6 percent of diesel demand, the study notes. More GMOs do not mean more food; instead, they make a mockery of the "Farmers Feed Cities" signs fronting massive mono-cropped fields. The rapid destruction of the world's greatest ecological treasure, the Amazon rainforest, continues apace as it is converted with bulldozers and chainsaws from the biodiverse lungs of the planet into endless acres of soybeans to feed, yes, cows and cars.

Big conventional farms around these parts were grossing several hundred dollars per acre, many times what they had grown content with. Cash crops were king. They wanted more land, fewer fencelines, bigger machinery. A land grab was in full tilt in our very midst, and many were happy to be bought up, bought off their land for a pretty little packet, which is small change to the big operators, of course. When land grabs scale up, sometimes exponentially around the world, what hope is there for the smallholder, the subsistence farmer, the peasant feeding his family, the biodynamic herbalist planting by the phases of the moon? Without soils, without seeds, we are lost. The further we stray from nature, the more lost we are. And you can bet that none of this is lost on the megalomaniacal monsters of the industrial food system along with their beholden researchers and investors, media and public relations teams, all busily advocating, funding the skewed studies and campaigns, rolling out the rapid genetic modification of the entire global food system, transforming our society into one big mass of chemical and genetic contamination. There is a definite sense of fair play that prevails in ultra-competitive professional sports like my beloved English football, but apparently not in Big Agra.

Thank goodness for small farmers and down-to-earth local markets where dedicated individuals and their families continue to come together, for now, to buy and sell pure, nutritious, fresh, local food that helps to keep them healthy and sane in a fast-paced world. They offer a happy, welcome alternative to the mass-produced, highly processed, nutritionally deficient, inadequately labelled offerings of the industrial food system.

Epilogue

During times of universal deceit, telling the truth becomes a revolutionary act. (George Orwell)

Alternative media and the Internet have opened up new channels for communicating and understanding current issues in fields that affect us all—politics, finance, food, farming, ecology, culture. However, competing and conflicting agendas make all media reports—from those perpetrated by the meekest of mainstream puppets to those coming from the most extreme conspiracy theorists—minefields to negotiate.

Many Native Americans are Idle No More. Grassroots protests like the Occupy movement find their voice and will in all likelihood continue to do so with increasing meaning and vehemence as a groundswell of disillusionment and frustration forms because of escalating prices, debt, corporate and government frauds, and deteriorating standards. Change has to come from the roots up, as consolidation of power at any cost appears to be the prime goal of the bald eagles on their lofty perch. A thorough shake-up is required since the problems facing us all are systemic and escalating. Failure to correct core cultural decadence, condescension and corruption at the top of society is already leading to colossal upheaval and revolt at the base as brutal impoverishment sucks ever more innocents into its orbit.

The Economics of Happiness is a project of the International Society for Ecology and Culture. Helena Norberg-Hodge is codirector and producer of *The Economics of Happiness*, a 68-minute documentary made by ISEC in 2011. http://www.theeconomicsofhappiness.org tells us:

> Economic globalization has led to a massive expansion in the scale and power of big business and banking. It has also worsened nearly every problem we face: fundamentalism and ethnic conflict; climate chaos and species extinction; financial instability and unemployment. There are personal costs too. For the majority of people on the planet life is becoming increasingly stressful. We have less time for friends and family and we face mounting pressures at work.
>
> *The Economics of Happiness* describes a world moving simultaneously in two opposing directions. On the one hand, government and big business continue to promote globalization and the consolidation of corporate power. At the same time, all around the world people are resisting those policies, demanding a re-regulation of trade and finance—and, far from the old institutions of power, they're starting to forge a very different future. Communities are coming together to rebuild more human scale, ecological economies based on a new paradigm—an economics of localization.

At local and community levels, successes can indeed be achieved by those able to hold on to personal freedoms and maintain independence from corporate and government bodies and resist their increasingly desperate methods of control. Those sufficiently outraged will flee Wall Street and Main Street, downsizing, retrenching, moving onto the land, taking up residence in simpler, more meaningful, deliberate lives. They will retire and retreat from the rat race, look back on it with scorn and maybe some shame and write their tell-all memoirs. They will source their shelter, occupations, food, culture and sustenance much closer to home. In doing so, they will be choosing to wrest back control of their own lives, to get back to living within their means. Most, however, will feel trapped, forced to continue in the way things are, to make do, to carry on carrying on, the way they have been conditioned to do, and they are likely to see their living standards, freedoms and rights eroded, their assets, property and dignity diminished. As for saving ourselves from getting sucked into ever more costly debts, conflicts and denials by which we ultimately self-destruct, it is difficult to envisage such an obvious goal when our main sources of information toe the corporate police-state line, promote skepticism and obfuscate the root causes and severity of the problems.

In one of his earliest public lectures, given in March 1948, E. F. Schumacher described the individual's task as twofold: first "to fully develop oneself," and second "to form one's relationship to other people—family, groups, one's countrymen, mankind—sensibly, ethically, or expressed quite simply, with joy."

In *Small Is Beautiful*, he argued first that the "natural capital" of earth's resources is irreplaceable. Global capitalism, squandering fossil fuels, threatens our civilization. Squander "the capital represented by living nature" and you "threaten life itself." To address the challenge of how to change humanity's relationship with the planet, Schumacher explained that society needs to mobilize a combination of "freedom and order," two apparently irreconcilable concepts. For Schumacher this meant "lots of small, autonomous units" committed to "the indivisibility of peace and also of ecology."

As each individual makes his and her own contribution and takes on responsibility, however small and seemingly futile, things move forward to a better place. Content in my chosen lifestyle, happy to be farming and living on the land with its ample rewards, my fervour may at times border on the delusional, but I honestly believe that our homes and farms can be seen as microcosms, generating food and energy, trading with the community, saving seeds, enhancing the soil, doing no harm, conserving the land to pass on to others to tend. In cooperating with like-minded folk, we shift the goalposts. Small solutions come into view. Critical mass then reorients thinking, aspirations gather collective momentum, and stubborn obstacles are cleared away. As anthropologist Margaret Mead noted wryly: "A small group of thoughtful people could change the world. Indeed, it's the only thing that ever has."

Eventually, mountains of baggage that held us back are removed and progress is achieved. Because people took a stand, slavery was nominally abolished, suffrage was established, and basic universal human rights and freedoms fostered. People *can* find a true voice; child and spousal abuse *can* be stamped out; apartheid, segregation and racism *can* be eradicated; people of different religions *can* live side by side; biodiversity *can* be conserved; nature *can* be respected; and even the shameful stain of war *can* be wiped off the face of the earth. This can likely only be achieved if the reins of our affairs are handed over to nurturing women before it's too late. "If we are going to have a future, it has to be a womanly future," Vandana Shiva says. Shining beacons of hope like Mahatma Gandhi, Martin Luther King and Nelson Mandela have been rare among men, true visionaries who dreamed such things and acted fearlessly on their dreams. Where are the enlightened leaders of today?

> *A human being is part of the whole called by us universe, a part limited in time and space. We experience ourselves, our thoughts and feelings as something separate from the rest. A kind of optical delusion of consciousness. This delusion is a kind of prison for us, restricting us to our personal desires and to affection for a few persons nearest to us. Our task must be to free ourselves from the prison by widening our circle of compassion to embrace all living creatures and the whole of nature in its beauty. The true value of a human being is determined by the measure and the sense in which they have obtained liberation from the self. We shall require a substantially new manner of thinking if humanity is to survive.* (Albert Einstein, 1954)

Appendix

Catalysts for Change

Spirited catalysts pass on knowledge and experience and reveal beauty and meaning in this world, thereby helping to keep us healthy in mind and body. Over recent years, I have learned so much from great doers and teachers. They have inspired me in my quest for insight into plants, soils, nutrition, health, growing, eating, cooking and living. The following people are some of these catalysts.

Food and Farming

Rudolf Steiner
(from http://en.wikipedia.org/wiki/Rudolf_SteinerWikipedia)

> After the First World War, Steiner became active in a wide variety of cultural contexts. He founded a number of schools, the first of which was known as the Waldorf school, and which later evolved into a worldwide school network. He also founded a system of organic agriculture,

now known as Biodynamic agriculture, which was one of the very first forms of, and has contributed significantly to the development of, modern organic farming. His work in medicine led to the development of a broad range of complementary medications and supportive artistic and biographic therapies. Homes for children and adults with developmental disabilities based on his work (including those of the Camphill movement) are widespread.

In 1924, a group of farmers concerned about the future of agriculture requested Steiner's help. Steiner responded with a lecture series on an ecological and sustainable approach to agriculture that increased soil fertility without the use of chemical fertilizers and pesticides. Steiner's agricultural ideas promptly spread and were put to the test internationally and Biodynamic agriculture is now practiced widely in Europe, North America, Asia, and Australasia.

A central aspect of biodynamics is that the farm as a whole is seen as an organism, and therefore should be a largely self-sustaining system, producing its own manure and animal feed. Plant or animal disease is seen as a symptom of problems in the whole organism. Steiner also suggested timing agricultural activities such as sowing, weeding, and harvesting to utilize the influences on plant growth of the moon and planets; and the application of natural materials prepared in specific ways to the soil, compost, and crops, with the intention of engaging non-physical beings and elemental forces. He encouraged his listeners to verify his suggestions empirically, as he had not yet done.

Dr. Vandana Shiva
Scientist, philosopher, feminist, author, environmentalist, activist, Dr. Vandana Shiva is a dynamic advocate for peace, sustainability and social justice.

(from http://www.thegreeninterview.com/vandana-shiva-bio)

Vandana Shiva was born in 1952 in Uttarakhand, India. Her father was a conservator of forests, and her mother was a farmer with a deep love for nature. Her parents were staunch supporters of Mahatma Gandhi, and Gandhi remains a profound influence on her thought. Echoing Gandhi, she says, "I have tried to be the change I want to see."

After receiving her schooling in India and training as a gymnast, Vandana Shiva earned a B.S. in Physics, an M.A. in the philosophy of science at the University of Guelph, and a PhD in nuclear physics at the University of Western Ontario. As a graduate student, however, she found herself troubled by the realization that science had "a dark side," and that she didn't know enough about the actual workings of society. India, she noted, had the third biggest scientific community in the world but remained "among the poorest of countries. Science and technology is supposed to create growth, remove poverty. Where is the gap?"

That question led her to study science policy at the Indian Institute of Science and the Indian Institute of Management in Bangalore where she explored interdisciplinary research in science, technology and environmental policy. She emerged as an authority in the field of environmental impact, and became deeply alarmed by the threat to biodiversity posed by biotechnology. Hearing the leaders of world agri-business describe their plan to control the world's supply of food and pharmaceuticals through the use of patented, genetically-engineered seeds, she founded the Research Foundation for Science, Technology and Ecology, dedicated to opposing such ventures.

In 1991, Dr. Shiva founded Navdanya, a national movement to protect the diversity and integrity of living resources, especially native seeds, and to oppose what she calls the colonization of life itself under the intellectual property and patent laws of the World Trade Organization agreement. Those laws, she says, have "only a negative function: to prevent others from doing their own thing; to prevent people from having food; to prevent people from having medicine; to prevent countries from having technological capacity." She describes these laws as a "tool for creating underdevelopment."

Dr. Shiva sees biodiversity as intimately linked to cultural diversity and knowledge diversity, and recently launched a global movement in support of bio-diversity and cultural diversity called Diverse Women for Diversity. In the 1970s, Dr Shiva was one of the original tree-huggers, the Chipko group of Indian women who surrounded trees to prevent them from being felled. Today, it would be fair to call her the world's most famous and effective advocate for bio-ethics, eco-feminism and bio-diversity.

Among Vandana Shiva's many honours is the Right Livelihood Award—also known as the "Alternative Nobel Prize"—for her work in placing women and ecology at the center of the international development agenda. She is the author of more than 300 papers in leading scientific and technical journals.

Joel Salatin, Polyface Farm
(from www.PolyfaceFarms.com)

In 1961, William and Lucille Salatin moved their young family to Virginia's Shenandoah Valley, purchasing the most worn-out, eroded, abused farm in the area near Staunton. Using nature as a pattern, they and their children began the healing and innovation that now supports three generations. Disregarding conventional wisdom, the Salatins planted trees, built huge compost piles, dug ponds, moved cows daily to enclosures of portable electric fencing and invented portable sheltering systems to produce all their animals on perennial prairie polycultures. Today the farm arguably represents America's premier nonindustrial food production oasis. Believing that the Creator's design is still the best pattern for the biological world, the Salatin family invites like-minded folks to join in the farm's mission: to develop emotionally, economically and environmentally enhancing agricultural enterprises and facilitate their replication throughout the world. The Salatins continue to refine their models to push environmentally friendly farming practices toward new levels of expertise.

Polyface Guiding Principles

Transparency. Anyone is welcome to visit the farm anytime. No trade secrets, no locked doors, every corner is camera-accessible.

Grass-based. Pastured livestock and poultry, moved frequently to new "salad bars," offer landscape healing and nutritional superiority.

Individuality. Plants and animals should be provided a habitat that allows them to express their physiological distinctiveness. Respecting and honoring the pigness of the pig is a foundation for societal health.

Community. We do not ship food. We should all seek food closer to home, in our food-shed, our own bioregion. This means enjoying seasonality and reacquainting ourselves with our home kitchens.

Nature's Template. Mimicking natural patterns on a commercial domestic scale ensures moral and ethical boundaries to human cleverness. Cows are herbivores, not omnivores; that is why we've never fed them dead cows like the United States Department of Agriculture encouraged (the alleged cause of mad cows).

Earthworms. We're really in the earthworm enhancement business. Stimulating soil biota is our first priority. Soil health creates healthy food.

I believe that to deal with the great unravelling taking place around us, we've got to come back home, immerse ourselves in that which goes on in our neighbourhoods and communities, in our own backyards or on the land we farm. We can feel paralyzed by the broader world scene, but we have enormous power in and around the places where we live.

(Michael Ableman, author of *Fields of Plenty*, speaking at the 2005 Bioneers Conference)

Natural Health

Dr. Samuel Epstein
(from http://www.preventcancer.com/about/epstein.htm)

Samuel S. Epstein, M.D., is professor emeritus of Environmental and Occupational Medicine at the University of Illinois School of Public Health, and Chairman of the Cancer Prevention Coalition. Dr. Epstein is an internationally recognized authority on avoidable causes of cancer, particularly unknown exposures to industrial carcinogens in air, water, the workplace, and consumer products—food, cosmetics and toiletries, and household products including pesticides—besides carcinogenic prescription drugs.

Derrick Jensen writes at http://thesunmagazine.org/archives/842?page=1: "Cancer prevention in this society has, according to Epstein, come to mean primarily two things: (1) stopping smoking; and (2) chemoprevention, such as taking the highly profitable prescription drug tamoxifen to try to prevent breast cancer. Sometimes it includes diet and exercise. But missing from most discussions of prevention—intentionally missing, says Epstein—is any mention of the probable cause of the current cancer epidemic: the poisoning of our entire planet.

It isn't really news that the air we breathe, the water we drink, and the foods we eat are all contaminated with carcinogens. Some toxicologists are predicting that the future of humankind could be slow suicide by poison. Yet, Epstein asserts, environmental toxins are ignored in cancer research, because reducing them doesn't serve the interests of chemical and pharmaceutical companies and the "cancer establishment"—mainly the National Cancer Institute and the American Cancer Society."

Dr. Shiv Chopra, author of *Corrupt to the Core*
(from www.shivchopra.com)

Shiv Chopra's name has become synonymous with food safety. He and fellow scientists have waged many battles over four decades against a succession of Canadian federal ministries of health and helped to protect the food supply worldwide. With support of his union, Dr. Chopra and his colleagues refused to approve various harmful drugs intended for meat and milk production. He endured disciplinary actions, spoke out publicly, testified at Senate committees, and won federal court cases against Health Canada. Due to Dr. Chopra's work, Bovine Growth Hormone was barred in Canada in 1999 and in the EU. He has spoken out on BGH, dangerous antibiotics like Revalor-H Baytril, and the true causes of mad cow disease.

In his *Five Pillars of Food Safety* address to Navdanya in New Delhi, India in 2008, Dr. Chopra observed: "There is enough food for everyone to eat but, as Mahatma Gandhi said, it will never be enough to satisfy greed. For instance, according to *The Economist* of August 2, 2008, the number of farmers in the United States is one million whereas in India it is two hundred million. Much of the food that those one million U.S. farmers produce is from pesticide dependent GMOs made by multinational corporations like Monsanto, DuPont, Pfizer, Syngenta, BASF, and others. Now, the farmers are being enticed to turn food crops into producing the so-called green fuel ethanol to cause road rage and climate change. The only solution to this madness is not to allow GMOs to produce any crops and cloned animals for food. Everything that people eat must be organically grown and the simplest way to do that is not to allow any of the following five substances from entering any food production:

- Hormones
- Antibiotics
- Rendered Dead Animal Wastes
- GMOs
- Pesticides/Herbicides.

GRASSROOTS ORGANIZATIONS

The organic movement

As an organic grower, farmer, and direct seller, I am interested to trace where organic culture came from, how it became a movement, how it has evolved, the challenges it faces today and its prospects for tomorrow.

(from http://en.wikipedia.org/wiki/Organic_movement)

> In the summer of 1924 Rudolf Steiner presented what has been called the first organic agriculture course to a group of over one hundred farmers and others at Koberwitz, now Kobierzyce, Poland. In Germany Rudolf Steiner's Spiritual Foundations for the Renewal of Agriculture, published in 1924, led to the popularization of biodynamic agriculture,

probably the first comprehensive organic farming system, that was based on Steiner's spiritual and philosophical teachings.

The first use of the term 'organic farming' is by Lord Northbourne (aka Walter James, 4th Baron Northbourne). The term derives from his concept of 'the farm as organism', which he expounded in his book, Look to the Land (1940), and in which he described a holistic, ecologically balanced approach to farming. Northbourne wrote of "chemical farming versus organic farming". http://www.orgprints.org/10138.

Sir Albert Howard's 1940 book, An Agricultural Testament, was influential in promoting organic techniques, and his 1947 book "The Soil and Health, A Study of Organic Agriculture" adopted Northbourne's terminology and was the first book to include 'organic' agriculture or farming in its title.

In 1939, strongly influenced by Sir Howard's work, Lady Eve Balfour launched the Haughley Experiment on farmland in England. It was the first, side-by-side comparison of organic and conventional farming. Four years later, she published The Living Soil, based on the initial findings of the Haughley Experiment. It was widely read, and lead to the formation of a key international organic advocacy group, the Soil Association.

During the 1950s, sustainable agriculture was a research topic of interest. The science tended to concentrate on the new chemical approaches. In the U.S., J.I. Rodale began to popularize the term and methods of organic growing. In addition to agricultural research, Rodale's publications through the Rodale Press helped to promote organic gardening to the general public.

In 1962, Rachel Carson, a prominent scientist and naturalist, published Silent Spring, chronicling the effects of DDT and other pesticides on the environment. A bestseller in many countries, including the US, and widely read around the world, Silent Spring was instrumental in the US government's 1972 banning of DDT. The book and its author are often credited with launching the environmental movement.

In the 1970s, worldwide movements concerned with environmental pollution caused by persistent agrichemical increased attention on organic farming. One goal of the organic movement was to promote consumption of locally grown food, which was promoted through slogans such as "Know Your Farmer, Know Your Food".

In 1972, the International Federation of Organic Agriculture Movements (IFOAM), was founded in Versailles, France. IFOAM was dedicated to the diffusion of information on the principles and practices of organic agriculture across national and linguistic boundaries.

In the 1980s, around the world, various farming and consumer groups began seriously pressuring for government regulation of organic production to ensure standards of production. This led to various legislation and certification standards being enacted through the 1990s and to date. Currently, most aspects of organic food production are government-regulated in the US and the European Union.

In the 2000s, the worldwide market for organic products (including food, beauty, health, bodycare, and household products, and fabrics) has grown rapidly.

Slow Food/Terra Madre
(from www.slowfood.com)

> Slow Food is a global, grassroots organization with supporters in 150 countries around the world who are linking the pleasure of good food with a commitment to their community and the environment.
>
> A non-profit member-supported association, Slow Food was founded in 1989 to counter the rise of fast food and fast life, the disappearance of local food traditions and people's dwindling interest in the food they eat, where it comes from, how it tastes and how our food choices affect the rest of the world.
>
> The **Terra Madre** network was launched by Slow Food to give a voice and visibility to the small-scale farmers, breeders, fishers and food artisans around the world whose approach to food production protects the environment and communities. The network brings them together with academics, cooks, consumers and youth groups so that they can join forces in working to improve the food system.
>
> The term food community refers to a group of these producers, defined by a place of origin and reflecting a

new idea of 'local economy' based on food, agriculture, tradition and culture. More than 2,000 Terra Madre food communities have been formed around the world.

The first world meeting of Terra Madre food communities was held in 2004 in Italy, and brought together 5,000 producers from 130 countries. The second edition in 2006 grew to include participation from 1,000 cooks, aware of their important role in supporting local, quality production, as well as 400 researchers and academics, seeking to bridge the theory of their work with hands-on knowledge. In 2008, 1,000 young producers, cooks, students and activists from around the world joined the network to show their commitment to ensuring traditions and agricultural wisdom is handed from one generation to the next.

National and regional Terra Madre networks have grown from the grassroots level and are working with Slow Food convivia to increase the capacity of local communities to provide good, clean and fair food. National Terra Madre meetings have been organized in many countries including Brazil, Sweden, Ireland, The Netherlands and Tanzania.

A wide variety of activities at the local level focus on sharing information and promoting better approaches to food production: from a group of South American academics working to promote eco-agriculture to an exchange between Ugandan and Kenyan farming communities or a bicycle tour of local small-scale farms in Canada.

Through these activities to strengthen and defend local food cultures, the Terra Madre family is growing every day, making the Slow Food concept of good, clean, and fair reality.

Internet resources

Dr. Joseph Mercola www.mercola.com The World's #1 Natural Health Website.

Natural News www.naturalnews.com Natural Health, Natural Living, Natural News.

Organic Consumers Association www.organicconsumers.org Campaigning for Health, Justice, Sustainability, Peace, and Democracy.

Gaia Health www.gaia-health.com Information for the health of you and your children.

Institute for Responsible Technology www.responsibletechnology.org The most comprehensive source of GMO health risk information on the web.

Non-GMO Project www.nongmoproject.org Working together to ensure the sustained availability of non-GMO food and products.

Bioneers www.bioneers.org Bioneers is inspiring a shift to live on Earth in ways that honor the web of life, each other, and future generations. Bioneers is a non-profit organization that highlights breakthrough solutions for restoring people and planet. Since 1990, Bioneers has served as a fertile hub of social and scientific innovators with nature-inspired approaches to the world's most pressing environmental and social challenges.

Orion Magazine www.orionmagazine.org "It is Orion's fundamental conviction that humans are morally responsible for the world in which we live, and that the individual comes to sense this responsibility as he or she develops a personal bond with nature." Orion's mission is to inform, inspire, and engage individuals and grassroots organizations in becoming a significant cultural force for healing nature and community.

The Weston A. Price Foundation www.westonaprice.org Dedicated to restoring nutrient-dense foods to the human diet through education, research and activism. It supports a number of movements that contribute to this objective including accurate nutrition instruction, organic and biodynamic farming, pasture-feeding of livestock, community-supported farms, honest and informative labeling, prepared parenting and nurturing therapies.

CPSIA information can be obtained at www.ICGtesting.com
Printed in the USA
LVOW100003040513

332250LV00001B/5/P